Quilting Your Style

Quilting Your Style

MAKE-IT-UNIQUE EMBELLISHING TECHNIQUES

Leah Fehr

Martingale®
& COMPANY

Quilting Your Style: Make-It-Unique
Embellishing Techniques
© 2009 by Leah Fehr

That Patchwork Place® is an imprint of
Martingale & Company®.

Martingale & Company
20205 144th Ave. NE
Woodinville, WA 98072-8478 USA
www.martingale-pub.com

Credits
President & CEO: Tom Wierzbicki

Editor in Chief: Mary V. Green

Managing Editor: Tina Cook

Technical Editor: Nancy Mahoney

Copy Editor: Marcy Heffernan

Design Director: Stan Green

Production Manager: Regina Girard

Illustrator: Laurel Strand

Cover & Text Designer: Stan Green

Photographer: Brent Kane

Printed in China
14 13 12 11 10 09   8 7 6 5 4 3 2 1

Library of Congress Cataloging-in-Publication Data
Library of Congress Control Number: 2009009474

ISBN: 978-1-56477-908-3

MISSION STATEMENT

Dedicated to providing quality products and service to inspire creativity.

Dedication

For my mom and my grandma

Acknowledgments

Thank you to:

The Sequin Team: Kathy, Jerdis, and Lisa, who with a 20-minute deadline sifted through the bag to find red and pink sequins and avoided getting little black ones stuck all over their hands.

My grandma whose enormous stash included many of the quilt backs, the thread, and some of the material for the quilt tops. I have always loved seeing what new old treasures we could discover at her and Grandpa's house.

My husband and my dad for their amazing support, even when they had no idea what a yo-yo or a bias strip was.

My mom for everything. From seamstress to courier to editor to support staff, she was there for every step of this process. I couldn't have done it without her.

Heidi Kaisand, Elizabeth Tisinger, and Jennifer Keltner for teaching me so much about quilt-instruction writing and for allowing me to be a part of their great team.

Penny Miller and Rosalie Davenport for all of their last-minute quilting and fabulous flexibility.

Karen Soltys, Nancy Mahoney, and everyone else at Martingale & Company for their time, know-how, and willingness to publish my first book.

Contents

THE PROJECTS

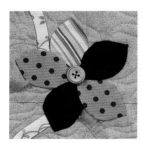

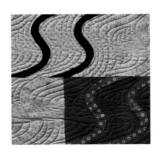

RUFFLES

BEADS

BUTTONS

SEQUINS

BUTTONS

APPLIQUÉ

EMBROIDERY

Quilting Your Style

The two of us went in and out of the large dressing rooms at Macy's, laughing loudly, then hushing ourselves only to laugh harder. We were trying on prom dress after prom dress. Some were serious choices—something we would actually wear in public. Others, well, we just wanted to see how it felt to wear something that poofy, or slinky, or short, or. . . . Maybe the fact that we were well out of high school and didn't really need to find one that fit was what made it so much fun.

I think, though, that I just like trying things on, be it a new outfit or a new sewing technique. I pick out a number of options, and then try them on to find out what works for me. That's the reason I decided to make "The Dressing-Room Sampler" on page 31. I wanted to try different embellishing techniques, but I didn't want the commitment of a whole quilt. The 5" blocks don't take a lot of time, but finishing each is enough to discover if you are successful in a technique and, most importantly, if you want to do it again.

What surprised me about the prom dress experience was what I liked when I came out of the dressing room. The sleek black dress I thought would be my number one choice wasn't, but the big poofy pink thing looked great. I discovered there are no rules determining what I would like and what would fit; I just have to try the options. Trying takes longer, but you come away knowing yourself and, in the case of sewing, your skills. You already modify a pattern by choosing colors different from those in the quilt in the photo, but you can truly make each quilt your own by adding different embellishments. This book will show you the possibilities, and my hope is that you will take it from there.

There are no rules about how your quilts should look, but you do need to follow a few rules concerning basic quiltmaking techniques to make your quilts turn out well. This book shows you new techniques and gives guidelines to encourage you to try something new and to help you develop the skills to make your own quilts with your own ideas. Where you go from here is up to you.

The Rules

Looking at a quilt, it's easy to think that there are a lot of rules associated with its assembly. To me, there are only a few that you really need to follow when you decide to make a quilt.

1. Enjoy what you're doing. A friend who worked with children always gave them a list of five rules where numbers 1 and 5 were, "Have fun." They thought it was funny—I think it's true. Quilting is a hobby; if you're ready to enjoy the process and learn something new, go on to number 2.

2. Use accurate ¼" seam allowances. They make your points sharp, your edges match, and most importantly, they make your blocks turn out the right size. If the ¼" line isn't already marked on your sewing machine, turn the handwheel on the side of the machine so the needle is all the way down. With a ruler, measure ¼" from the needle and mark the seam allowance on the bed of the machine with a piece of masking tape. Be careful not to cover the feed dogs on your sewing machine. Use several layers of masking tape, building a raised edge to guide your fabric.

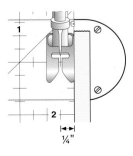

Cut three strips of fabric, each 1½" x 5". Sew them together along their long edges using the ¼" seam guide you just marked on your machine. Press and measure the width of the three-strip unit; the center strip should be exactly 1" wide. If it's not, adjust your ¼" guide accordingly until you find the correct width. Practice until you can sew a ¼" seam allowance consistently.

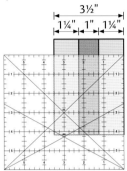

3. Press, don't iron. After sewing pieces together, take the time to press the seam allowances flat. The quilt instructions will tell you which way to press your seam allowances to make the quilt go together easily. If you press your seam allowances directly after sewing, your quilt will lie flat and keep its dimensions. The difference between pressing and ironing is small but important. When pressing, you hold the iron down on top of your pieces. When ironing, you move the iron back and forth across the fabric. Ironing can warp the seams. Pressing will keep them straight. Also, turn off the steam on your iron when you're pressing your quilt. Steam can warp your pieces and seams too.

4. Make good quilts with good tools. Follow the instructions in your sewing machine's manual on how and when to clean it.

Most quilters use a large cutting mat, a rotary cutter, and an acrylic ruler to cut their fabric.

These tools allow for fast and accurate cuts. They're expensive to purchase when you start quilting, but with proper care, they will last for years.

A good quilting reference book should also be in your arsenal. In this book you'll find instructions and tips to make all of the quilts, but it's always best to have a number of resources when you're learning something new.

5. Have fun. Did you think it could be anything else?

THE RULES YOU CAN BREAK

The rebel in us all wants to break some rules along the way. In quilting, as long as you keep the foundation of good construction in your quilts, you're free to change any perceived rule to make your project fit your style. Break these five first, and then start finding your own to change.

1. Make quilts from 100% cotton only. I love strolling through quilt stores. I touch each bolt of material and try out my own color combinations. I enjoy the feel of 100% cotton, and most of my quilts are made exclusively of it. But quilts don't always have to be made of cotton, especially if they're trendy and not intended to be heirlooms. Cotton is held in high esteem for quilts because of its feel and durability. The weave of the fabric is such that a needle will pass through it without breaking or damaging the fibers. Other types of fabrics don't have this resilience, and with the numerous times a needle passes through the fabric of a quilt, the fibers can fray and develop holes. Cautionary tales aside, if other fabrics, such as delicate silks or durable denim, are used as embellishments or only in certain sections of a quilt top, they can add depth and texture to the overall quilt that cotton cannot. If you love a material, don't let its percentage of cotton determine if you'll use it in your quilt.

2. Stick to predesigned patterns. You can find a quilt pattern anywhere, not just in books or magazines. It seems a little counterproductive for a book of quilt patterns to point this out, but patterns are everywhere, from the layout of sidewalk bricks to the design on a piece of china. As long as you've got graph paper and a pencil, you can create simple quilts that, made with the fabrics you love, can be stunning. It's easier, of course, to search through quilt patterns that have already been created to find something you would like to make, but don't discount your eye and your ability to find patterns you love.

3. Don't change the size of your project. The math isn't that tricky. A piece of paper, a pencil, and probably a calculator are all you need to change the size of any quilt pattern. The fabric you buy is typically listed as being 44" to 45" wide. To allow for discrepancies and to trim off the tight edges of fabric on each side (called selvages), assume that each piece you buy will end up being 42" wide.

Look at the size of the pieces in one block. Is the block a 12" square like in "Whirlwind Romance" on page 63? If you'd like to make that pattern into a 90"-square queen-size quilt, just divide 90 by 12 (90 ÷ 12 = 7.5). Seven 12" blocks will give you 84" total (7 x 12 = 84). If you add a 3" border to all sides of your quilt, the total will be 90" (84 + 6 = 90). You'll need seven rows of seven blocks each for your queen-size quilt, which equals 49 blocks (7 x 7 = 49), or in this instance, 49 squares.

Next, to determine how much fabric you need for your queen-size quilt, divide the width of fabric by the size of the cut piece. If your fabric is 42" wide and the cut piece is 12½" square (12" + ½" for seam allowances): 42 ÷ 12.5 = 3.36 squares per 42" strip of fabric. Round this *down* to 3 squares. Divide the number of squares you need by the number of squares per 42" strip: 49 ÷ 3 = 16.33. Round this number *up* to 17. This is the number of strips you'll need to cut 49 squares. (If you cut 16 strips, you'll only get 48 squares.) Then, multiply the number of strips by the size of the cut squares: 17 x 12.5" = 212.5". Finally, divide the total number of inches by the number of inches in a yard (which is 36): 212.5 ÷ 36 = 5.9. Round this *up* to the next standard yardage measurement. In this example, you'd need 6 yards of fabric to make your queen-size quilt. You know yourself and your cutting skills. If you want to allow for cutting errors, allow yourself another 12½" strip of fabric, and purchase 6½ yards of fabric. Remember you'll also need to figure additional yardage for the embellishments.

4. Make a quilt for future generations. Quilts can take a lot of time, but not every one has to be an heirloom. Instead of buying a throw from a catalog, you can make a lap quilt to curl up with on the couch. Instead of a new tablecloth, you can make a runner to lie across the tablecloth you already have. Quilt a 5" block and use it as a coaster. Use the math skills you learned in rule 3 to make a wall hanging just the right size for that tricky wall next to the stairs. You can custom make a quilt to soften any space in your home, not just your beds.

5. Wait until you've retired to take up quilting. While waiting out a five-hour layover in Newark Airport, I pulled out my latest redwork embroidery project and began to stitch. The little boy next to me stopped playing with his toy truck, watched me for awhile, then stage whispered to his dad, "What is she doing?" The father responded, "She's stitching, just like Grandma does." Not married at the time, I was quite removed from becoming a grandmother anytime soon, and the comment upset me. Stitching and quilting can be for older women. It can be for younger women. It can be for men or children—anyone who wants to make something unique with his or her own hands. It's relaxing and worth the extra time it takes to do it yourself.

The Basics

No matter what your skill level or experience, this section will tell you everything you need to know to make the quilts in this book.

Rotary Cutting

1. Making sure that your fabric is smooth and without wrinkles, fold the fabric in half, matching the selvages. Lay the fabric on a mat with the fold nearest you; be sure there are no twists along the fold and the fabric is smooth underneath. Align a square ruler with the fold of the fabric and place your longest straight ruler to the left of the square so that the raw edges of the fabric are covered. (Reverse this procedure if you are left-handed.)

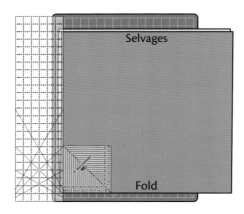

Selvages

Fold

2. Set the square ruler aside, and then cut along the right edge of the long ruler. Be sure to roll the rotary cutter away from you. Remove the long ruler and gently remove the waste strip.

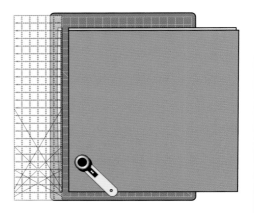

3. Align the ruler to the desired strip width from the cut edge of the fabric and carefully cut a strip. For example, to cut 2"-wide strips, place the 2" mark on the edge of the fabric. Continue cutting strips until you have the required number of strips. Periodically stop and square up your fabric edge again before continuing.

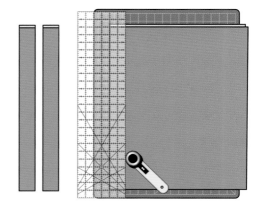

To cut squares and rectangles, cut strips in the required widths. Using a small ruler (typically 6" x 6" or 6" x 12") and placing the ruler on the left as before, trim the selvage ends of the strips. You are ready to cut pieces as required.

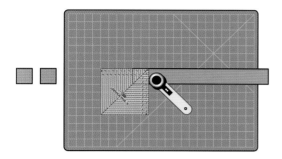

Cutting Bias Strips

To make pieces that can be curved for appliqué, the fabric must be cut on the bias—at a 45° angle to the selvage of your fabric. To cut bias strips, you'll need a rotary-cutting ruler with a 45° line. Lay the fabric flat with the right side facing up on a cutting mat. Align the 45° line on the ruler with a selvage edge of the fabric as shown.

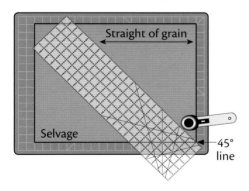

Cut along the ruler edge to make a large triangle. To cut strips, use the edge of the first cut as a guide, and align the desired strip-width measurement (as specified in your project) on the ruler with the cut edge of the fabric. Cut the number of strips required for the project you

are making. To cut the longest strips possible, alternate cutting strips from the long sides of each piece.

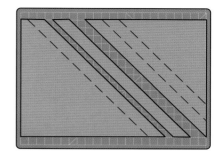

Making Templates

Since you'll be making more than one of each appliqué piece, you'll find it handy to make a plastic template for each pattern piece. Templates made from clear or frosted plastic are durable and accurate. Because you can see through the plastic, you can easily trace the shapes from the patterns. You can trace the pieces of each appliqué design directly from the pattern to create the templates you'll need. Seam allowances are not included on templates for appliqué pieces. Prepare your templates accurately to ensure the best results.

To make the templates, place template plastic over each pattern piece and trace with a fine-line permanent marker, making sure to trace the lines exactly. Do not add a seam allowance. Use utility scissors to cut out the templates, cutting exactly on the drawn lines. You need only one plastic template for each different pattern piece.

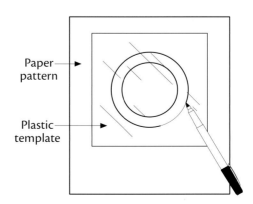

FUSIBLE APPLIQUÉ

Fusible appliqué is a fast and easy way to prepare appliqué shapes using fusible web. Fusible web is available with smooth paper on one side and adhesive on the reverse, or with paper on both sides and an adhesive in the middle. When you purchase a fusible-web product, take time to read the manufacturer's directions. Different products call for different heat settings and handling instructions.

1. Make a plastic template for each appliqué shape as described in "Making Templates" on page 17; then trace around the shapes as many times as needed onto the paper-backed side of the fusible web, leaving about ½" between shapes. Or if you prefer, you can simply trace each shape directly from the pattern onto the paper backing of the fusible web, eliminating the need to make plastic templates. However, I find that drawing around a plastic template is actually quicker and more accurate when I need multiple shapes to be identical.

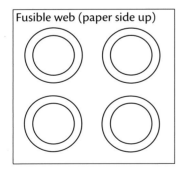

2. Roughly cut the shape out of the fusible web, leaving about ¼" margin around the marked line.

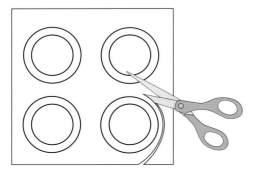

3. Place the shape fusible-web side down on the wrong side of the appropriate appliqué fabric. Following the manufacturer's directions, iron in place.

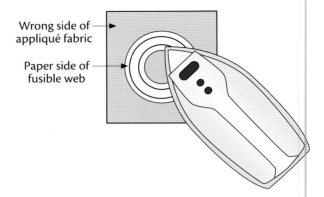

4. Cut out the fabric shape on the traced lines and remove the paper backing.

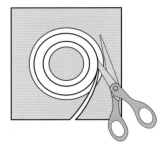

5. Position the appliqué shape, adhesive side down, on the right side of the background fabric. Once you're satisfied with how the appliqués look, press in place.

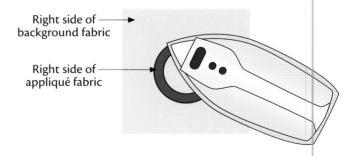

6. When all the pieces are fused, finish the edges with a decorative stitch, such as a modified chain stitch. For detailed instructions, refer to "Modified Chain Stitch" on page 22.

Starch Appliqué

For this method, you'll need a can of spray starch, a small cup or dish, and cotton swabs.

1. Using heat-resistant template plastic and referring to "Making Templates" on page 17, make a plastic template for the appliqué piece. Cut out the template on the traced line so that it is the exact size of the pattern piece.

2. Place the plastic template on the wrong side of the chosen fabric. Using the plastic template as a guide, draw approximately ¼" outside the edges of the template using a pencil or permanent pen. Cut out the shape, cutting on the drawn line. Draw the shape the number of times indicated on the pattern.

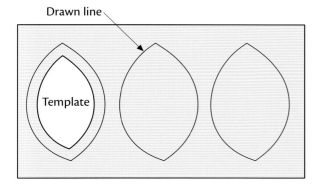

Drawn line

Template

3. Place the appliqué shape flat, with the wrong side up, on your ironing board. Center the plastic template on the appliqué shape. Spray a small amount of starch into a cup. Dip a cotton swab in the starch and wet the exposed seam allowance with starch.

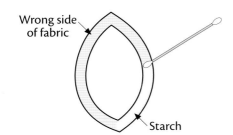

Wrong side of fabric

Starch

4. With a dry iron and using the plastic template as a guide, press the seam allowance over the edge of the plastic template, creating a fabric shape the size of the template. Allow the piece to cool and carefully remove the template. Turn the shape over and press the right side of the fabric shape.

Smooth Edges

Keep your appliqué shapes free of bumps by gliding the iron along the sides of the plastic template rather than folding the seam allowance over the template bit by bit. To do this, gently lift up one part of the seam allowance and place the iron behind it; then using the iron, fold the seam allowance over the template in one motion to create the smoothest edge.

Embellishing Your Quilt

Here are the techniques I used to embellish the quilts in this book. Refer to this section when indicated in the quilt instructions.

Folded Seams

1. On the right side of a fabric rectangle, place small marks (about ⅛" long) in the seam allowance on each long side of the rectangle as indicated in the project instructions. For example, on a 5½" x 7½" rectangle, place marks at the 1½", 3", 4½", and 6½" points, as shown.

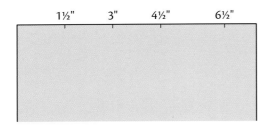

2. On the wrong side of the marked rectangle, lay the ⅛" wooden dowel on the 1½" marks. (If you don't have ⅛" wooden dowel, you can also use a wooden food skewer or a ¼" bias pressing bar.) Fold and pin the rectangle around the dowel so the marks are aligned on the back of the dowel as shown.

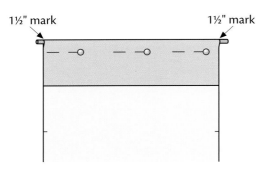

3. Resting the presser foot on top of the dowel, sew ⅛" from the edge of the dowel using its straight edge as a guideline as shown. Do not sew right next to the edge of the dowel, because that will make the fabric too tight, and it will be difficult to remove the dowel. Remove the dowel from the sewn fold. Press the sewn fold to one side. The sewn fold should be ¼" wide.

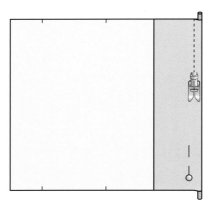

4. Repeat steps 2 and 3 for all the parallel marks on the marked rectangle. Press the sewn folds in the same direction directly after sewing each fold.

Ruffles

1. For this technique you need to cut 1"-wide rectangles (or strips) the length specified in the project instructions. Cut the number of rectangles specified for the project you are making. Adjust the stitch length on your sewing machine to its longest stitch setting. Using matching thread, sew a straight line down the center of each rectangle, leaving at least a 2" tail of thread at each end for gathering the fabric.

2. Holding onto the threads at one end of the rectangle, pull on one of the two threads at the other end to gather the rectangle to the length indicated for the project.

3. Pin the ruffle to the background square. Topstitch the ruffle using matching thread.

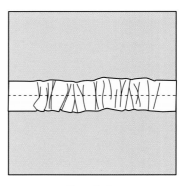

Topstitch.

Yo-Yos

1. Make a plastic template for the yo-yo circle as described in "Making Templates" on page 17; then trace around the circle onto the wrong side of the chosen fabric. Trace the circle the number of times indicated on the pattern, leaving about ½" between circles. Cut out the circles, cutting on the drawn line. Thread a needle and knot the end. Turn under the edge of each circle ¼" onto the wrong side of the fabric and finger-press. Insert the needle between the wrong sides of the fabric as shown.

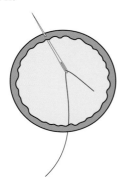

2. Sew a running stitch close to the folded edge of the circle, spacing the stitches about ⅛" apart. When you have stitched completely around the circle, pull up the thread tightly to gather the circle edge as shown. Make a couple of tiny stitches in the gathered folds to secure the thread. The yo-yo gathered side is the right side.

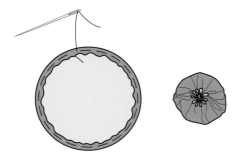

Embroidery Stitches

I used the stitches described here for the hand embroidery on the quilts in this book. To make each of the stitches you'll need 6-ply embroidery floss or pearl cotton, as well as a small embroidery hoop. Use a water-soluble marker to draw any lines. Before pressing the finished embroidery, be sure to spray the lines with water so they disappear.

Zigzag Stitch

Draw two parallel lines ¼" apart. Using two strands of embroidery floss, bring the needle up at A, near the end of one parallel line. Insert the needle at B (about ¼" from A) on the second line, creating a diagonal stitch. Come up at C, go down at B, then come back up at C and go down at D. Repeat the stitch, alternating sides along the parallel lines.

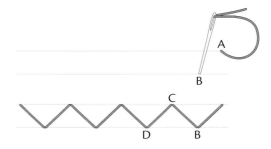

Coral Stitch

Draw a line. Using three strands of floss and starting at the end of the line, bring the needle up at A. Hold the floss down with your left thumb on the line and make a small stitch ½" to the left under the floss from B to C; pull the needle through the loop and over the floss. Pull to make a knot. Make the next stitch in the same way, moving to the left.

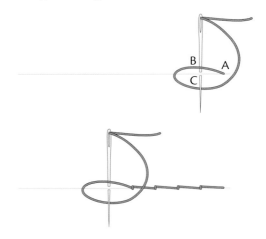

Modified Chain Stitch

Draw a line. Using four strands of embroidery floss (or two strands of size 5 pearl cotton) and starting at the end of the line, bring the needle up at A. Insert the needle at B, about ½" from A. Make a small stitch, bringing the needle up at C, as shown, keeping two strands on each side of the needle. Repeat to cover the marked line, keeping all of the stitches even.

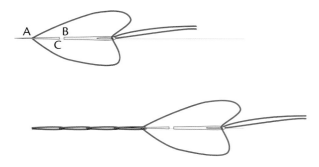

Split Stitch

Using four strands of embroidery floss, bring the needle up at A along the edge of the appliqué circle, ensuring you catch the appliqué fabric in the stitch. Working in a clockwise direction, insert the needle at B, about ¼" from A. Make a small stitch, bringing the needle up at C, as shown, keeping two strands on each side of the needle. Repeat to stitch around the circle, keeping all of the stitches even.

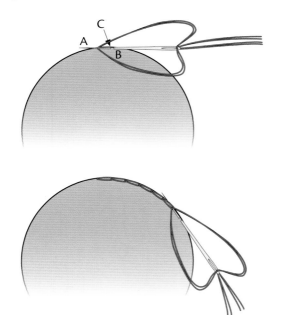

BORDERS

When all the blocks are complete and sewn together as directed in the project instructions, you are ready to add borders. The border-strip lengths given in the project instructions are based on the dimensions of the pieces after sewing an accurate ¼"-wide seam allowance. As each quilter's seam allowance may vary slightly, be sure to measure your quilt top as directed below to cut border strips the length you need.

To find the correct measurement for the border strips, always measure the quilt top through the center. This ensures that the borders are of equal length and helps keep your quilt square. If the quilt is larger than the length of one strip, you will need to sew the strips together with a diagonal seam as described in step 1 and 2 of "Binding" on page 25. Then cut strips the required length from the longer strip.

1. Measure the length of your quilt top through the center. Cut two border strips to this length, piecing as necessary. Mark the centers of the border strips and the quilt top edges. Pin the borders to the quilt top, matching centers and ends, easing if necessary. Sew the borders in place with a ¼"-wide seam allowance. Press the seam allowance toward the border strip, unless instructed otherwise.

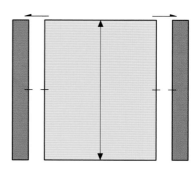

Mark centers. Measure center
of quilt, top to bottom.

2. Measure the width of the quilt top through the center, including the just-added side borders. Cut two border strips to this measurement, piecing as necessary. Mark, pin, sew in place, and press the border strips in the same manner as before. Repeat this method for each additional border.

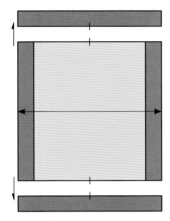

Mark centers. Measure center of quilt, side to side, including borders.

Quilt Sandwich

A quilt is made up of three components—that's what makes it different from a blanket. The top is the layer most people think of as the quilt, the part you've sewn together using a pattern.

The middle layer is the batting. Batting comes in different lofts (high being the thickest and low being the thinnest) and is made of different materials, cotton, polyester, and wool among the options. To determine which loft and material to use in a quilt, you have to feel all of the options and decide what you like the best and what works the best for your quilt. Professional machine quilters and quilt stores have the most variety of batting; larger craft store chains may have only a few choices.

The bottom layer is the backing. The quilt backing should be at least 6" larger than the quilt top (3" on all sides) for ease in quilting and in squaring up the quilt. For quilts between 36" and 60" wide, sewing together two pieces of fabric the width of the quilt top with a horizontal seam is the best use of fabric. For quilts wider than 60", one or two vertical seams is best. When piecing the backing, be sure to trim off the selvages before sewing the pieces together. The selvages are so tightly woven that they can cause the sewing needle to jump or miss a stitch when machine quilting. Press the seam allowance open to reduce bulk.

If you decide to use a professional machine quilter, your job is finished after you sew the top and backing and choose the type of batting and thread color you'd like. If you decide to finish your quilt yourself, you must first make a quilt sandwich. To do this, first spread your backing wrong side up on a large, flat surface, smoothing all wrinkles. Tile or wood floors work the best. Use masking tape to tape all four edges of the backing so it is taut and wrinkle free. Don't pull on the backing too much or it will be distorted. When you remove the tape, you don't want the edges to spring back a couple of inches, but instead to stay where they are.

Center the batting over the backing, smoothing out all wrinkles. Make sure the batting is flat, being careful not to stretch it. Place the quilt top, right side up, on top of the batting, aligning the center of the quilt with the center of the backing. Smooth out all wrinkles, working from the center to the outer edges, again taking care not to stretch the quilt out of shape. You should have at least 3" of backing and batting extending beyond your quilt top on all four sides. Now you have a quilt sandwich.

Basting

Whether you baste your quilt with a needle and thread or use safety pins to temporarily hold the three layers together is a personal preference. The purpose behind both techniques is to keep the quilt sandwich together so it doesn't shift as you quilt. If you plan to machine quilt your quilt at home, you might want to choose pin basting because you can easily open and remove the pins as you approach them.

For thread basting, use a large needle and strong white thread to make long running stitches toward one corner of the quilt, making sure you go through all three layers. Repeat, basting to each corner to make an X through the quilt. Continue basting the remainder of the quilt in a grid pattern, making sure the stitching lines are no more than 6" apart. Once you are finished quilting, use your seam ripper to remove the basting stitches.

For pin basting, insert 1"-long safety pins to secure all three layers. Begin pinning at the center of the quilt, working your way to the outer edges. Place pins 5" to 6" apart in rows. When closing the pins, take care not to bunch up the backing fabric.

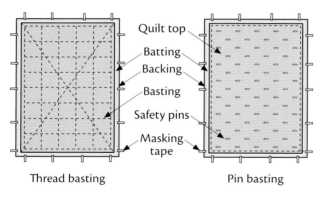

Thread basting   Pin basting

Quilt top
Batting
Backing
Basting
Safety pins
Masking tape

MACHINE QUILT, HAND QUILT, OR TIE

Quilting—whether by hand or machine—permanently secures the layers of the quilt together. For the best results, no unquilted space should exceed 6" x 6" on the quilt surface, or the batting might fall apart and bunch to one side. I'm sure you've seen store-bought comforters that after a couple of washings turn out like this.

This book gives instructions for three ways to finish your quilt. There are quilt books devoted to teaching hand- and machine-quilting techniques, and they provide quilting patterns.

Please look to a variety of sources for more information about these techniques.

Machine quilting is using your sewing machine to quilt the layers of your quilt together and is suitable for any type and size of quilt. It allows you to complete a project quickly and doesn't require a special machine. For stitching straight lines and gentle curves, it's extremely helpful to have a walking foot. This attachment will evenly feed the layers through the machine without the fabric shifting or puckering.

A common machine-quilting technique is free-motion quilting. You need a darning foot and the ability to drop the feed dogs on your machine or to cover them. (The feed dogs are the metal spikes under your presser foot that move the fabric as you sew.) With free-motion quilting, you don't turn the fabric under the needle, but instead guide the fabric in the direction of the design. Because the feed dogs are lowered, the stitch length is determined by the speed at which you run the machine and feed the fabric under the foot. To free-motion quilt, start in the middle of your project and work toward the edges, making curves fit into each other without intersecting. When you machine quilt, you'll probably need to roll the quilt, leaving flat only the small area you are working on so that the quilt is easier to grasp and move under the presser foot. The majority of the quilts in this book are machine quilted.

Walking foot attachment   Darning foot

Free-motion quilting designs

Hand quilting is, of course, quilting the three layers together by hand. You'll need a quilting hoop and a removable (water- or air-soluble) marker or chalk to mark the quilting design, if desired. A quilting hoop holds the layers of your quilt taut so that they don't shift during quilting. Hoops are available in a variety of sizes and models. Hand quilting can take a long time, but it is very satisfying. You can use small even stitches and quilting thread or a large running stitch and pearl cotton, depending on the look you're hoping to achieve. Anything goes as long as you remember to leave no areas larger than 6" x 6" unquilted.

Tying is another method of finishing. You can use pearl cotton, yarn, or any thicker thread for ties. If you use pearl cotton or thinner yarn, use two or more lengths to make a more substantial tie. As with machine or hand quilting, you'll need to baste your quilt top and space the ties no more than 6" apart. I tied "Cord of Woods" on page 43 to show how a tied quilt looks. It's up to you whether you like the ties to show on the front or on the back. For my quilt, I placed the ties on the back to give a design to both sides. I recommend using a polyester or cotton/poly blend batting for a tied quilt; it gives the quilt a nice loft and is easier to use.

To tie a quilt, I start by cutting out a square of thin cardboard, from a cereal box for example, to measure the distance between ties. In this case I made a 5½" square cardboard ruler.

Thread a long needle with an 18" length of yarn or pearl cotton. Starting in the quilt center, insert the needle through all three layers, leaving about a 1" tail of thread. Bring the needle up ¼" from the tail as shown.

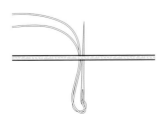

To make a knot, holding the tail, wrap the needle behind the tail and through the loop. Pull the ends tight; wrap the left tail around the right tail and tighten again. Trim the ends even, about ½" long.

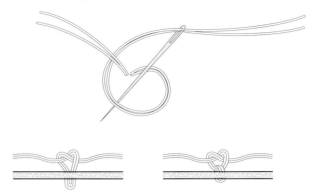

Align one corner of the cardboard ruler with the first tie. You can place three more ties equal distance apart by sewing the ties next to the remaining three corners of the ruler.

Binding

Before you can add the binding to your quilt, you'll need to square up the quilt. This means you need to trim the layers to make an even, straight edge. To square up your quilt, lay it flat on a cutting mat, measure from a fixed point, such as a seam line of a border or block, and trim the excess batting and backing even with the quilt top. Using a fixed point as a marker ensures that each edge is one straight line, which is important when sewing on the binding and for the structure of your quilt.

The width of binding is a personal preference and can vary from 2" to 2½" wide. It's even possible to use 2¾" strips if you like a wider binding or are using a thicker batting. I prefer a smaller binding, so I used 2¼" strips, cut across the width of fabric, for the quilts in this book. If you want a wider binding, remember you'll need a little more fabric than called for in the project instructions. When sewing your binding strips together, use a diagonal seam to reduce bulk.

1. Lay the strips at right angles with right sides together. Using a pencil and a ruler, mark a diagonal line from corner to corner, as shown.

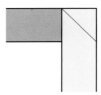

2. Sewing exactly on the marked line, join the strips to make one long piece of binding. Trim the excess fabric, leaving a ¼" seam allowance. Press the seam allowances open.

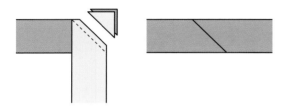

3. Fold the strip in half lengthwise, wrong sides together, and press.

4. Along one side of the quilt, not at a corner, align the raw edge of the strip with the raw edge of the quilt. Beginning 12" from the end of the strip and using a ¼"-wide seam allowance, stitch the binding to the quilt. Stop ¼" from the first corner and backstitch.

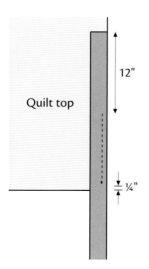

Quilt top

12"

¼"

5. Cut the threads and remove the quilt from the sewing machine. Fold the binding straight up and away from the quilt so the fold forms a 45° angle.

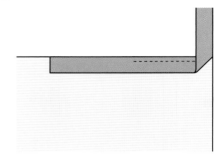

6. Holding the 45° fold in place, fold the binding back onto itself, even with the edge of the quilt to create an angled pleat at the corner. Begin with a backstitch at the fold of the binding and continue stitching along the edge of the quilt, mitering each corner in the same way.

7. Stop stitching about 6" from the starting end of the binding strip and backstitch. Remove the quilt from the machine. Overlap the beginning and ending tails of the binding. Mark the overlap by the same distance as your binding strips are wide. In this case, mark a 2¼" overlap. Trim each end of the binding at the marked points.

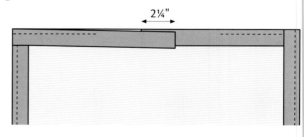

2¼"

8. Open the folds of the two ends of the binding and overlap the ends at right angles, right sides together as shown. Pin the ends together and draw a seam line diagonally between the points where the strips intersect.

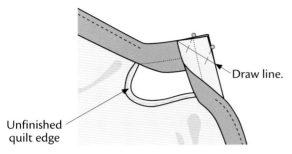

Draw line.

Unfinished quilt edge

9. Sew the binding ends together along the drawn line. Trim the excess fabric, leaving a ¼" seam allowance. Finger-press the seam allowances open.

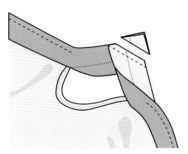

10. Refold the binding in half, finger-press, and sew it in place on the quilt.

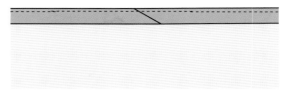

Complete stitching.

11. Fold the binding to the back of the quilt so that it covers the machine stitching. Hand stitch in place, mitering the corners as you reach them.

Quilt back

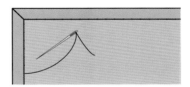

The Projects

Try 12 different embellishing techniques with minimal commitment on this colorful sampler wall hanging.

Pieced by Leah Fehr and machine quilted by Penny Miller
Finished quilt: 45½" x 45½" • Finished block: 5" x 5"

The Dressing-Room Sampler

MATERIALS

Yardage is based on 42"-wide fabric.

1½ yards of light blue print for blocks and outer border

⅞ yard of pink striped fabric for blocks, appliqués, sashing, inner border, and binding

⅝ yard of brown print for appliqués, middle border, and yo-yos

18" x 22" piece (fat quarter) of cream-and-blue print for appliqués

10" x 10" square of pink dotted fabric for appliqués and yo-yos

10" x 10" square of cream floral for appliqués and ruffles

5½" x 5½" square of brown silk for center block

3¼ yards of fabric for backing

52" x 52" piece of batting

5" x 5" square of fusible web

2" x 3" rectangle of heat-resistant template plastic

5½" x 5½" square of iron-on stabilizer

60 assorted round gold, brown, and pink beads in various sizes

20 assorted green, blue, pink, brown, and cream buttons (⅜" to ½" diameter)

2 matching tan buttons (about ⅜" diameter) for flower centers in outer border

60 assorted pink, white, blue, clear, silver, and gold sequins (⅛" to ⅜" diameter)

Cream, brown, metallic silver, and gray thread

1 skein *each* of blue, pink, yellow, cream, and brown embroidery floss

1 skein of gray novelty yarn

Water-soluble pen

Pencil or chalk marker

⅜" bias pressing bar

⅛"-diameter wooden dowel

PREPARING APPLIQUÉ SHAPES

Referring to "Fusible Appliqué" on page 18 and using the patterns on page 41, trace five of pattern B and four of pattern C onto the paper side of fusible web. Cut the fusible web pieces out and fuse one B and one C onto the brown print, two B onto the cream floral, two B and one C onto cream-and-blue print, one C onto the pink striped fabric, and one C onto the pink dotted fabric. Referring to "Starch Appliqué" on page 19 and using pattern D, prepare two pink striped, four brown print, and four pink dotted petals (10 total).

Cutting

From the *lengthwise* grain of the pink striped fabric, cut:

4 rectangles, 2½" x 9½"

From the remaining pink striped fabric, cut:

5 binding strips, 2¼" x 42"

4 strips, 2½" x 21½"

8 rectangles, 2½" x 5½"

2 pattern D, prepared for starch appliqué

1 pattern C, prepared with fusible web

From the light blue print, cut:

4 border strips, 8½" x 42"

1 rectangle, 5½" x 7½"

7 squares, 5½" x 5½"

From the cream floral, cut:

3 rectangles, 1" x 10"

2 pattern B, prepared with fusible web

From the brown print, cut:

4 border strips, 3½" x 42"

3 pattern A

4 pattern D, prepared for starch appliqué

1 pattern B, prepared with fusible web

1 pattern C, prepared with fusible web

From the pink dotted fabric, cut:

3 pattern A

4 pattern D, prepared for starch appliqué

1 pattern C, prepared with fusible web

From the cream-and-blue print, cut:

4 bias strips, 1½" x approximately 24½"★

2 pattern B, prepared with fusible web

1 pattern C, prepared with fusible web

★To cut the longest strips possible, cut two strips from the long edges of each triangle. Refer to "Cutting Bias Strips" on page 17 as needed.

Mitered Square Block

1. Following the manufacturer's instructions, press the square of iron-on stabilizer to the wrong side of the brown silk square. (An iron-on stabilizer works best for silky fabrics because it gives them stability without making them too stiff. The stabilizer strengthens the fabric so the edges don't stretch when you're sewing.)

2. On the wrong side of the brown silk square, using a pencil or chalk marker, mark each corner ¼" from the raw edge as shown in preparation for making mitered corners.

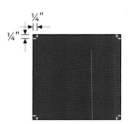

3. Fold the brown silk square in half, right sides together, vertically and horizontally. Finger-press to mark the center of each side as shown.

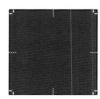

4. Fold each pink striped 2½" x 9½" rectangle in half, wrong sides together. Finger-press one side to mark the center as shown.

5. With right sides together, place the brown silk square on top of a rectangle, matching the center creases as shown; pin in place. Pin a rectangle on the opposite side of the square in the same manner.

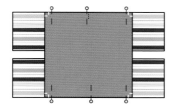

6. With the brown silk square on top, sew the rectangles to the square, starting and stopping at the ¼" marks with a small backstitch. Press the seam allowances toward the square.

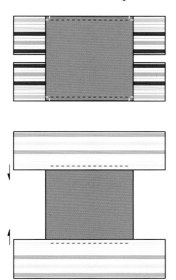

7. Repeat steps 5 and 6 to sew the remaining two rectangles to the square. The unstitched ends of the rectangle will extend beyond the square.

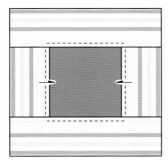

8. Fold the brown silk square in half diagonally, right sides together, and align the edges of the rectangles as shown. Draw a diagonal line from the corner of the rectangle to the seam line. Stitch exactly on the marked line, sewing from the inner corner to the outer edge to make a mitered corner. Trim the seam allowances to ¼" and press the seam allowances to one side.

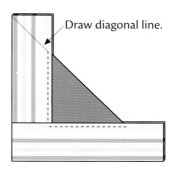
Draw diagonal line.

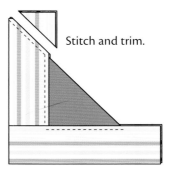
Stitch and trim.

9. Miter the remaining corners in the same manner. The block should measure 9½" square, including seam allowances.

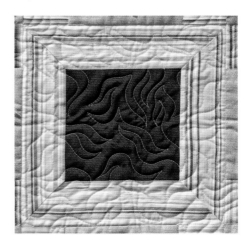

Folded Seams

Refer to "Folded Seams" on page 19 for detailed instructions.

1. On the right side of the light blue rectangle, mark each long side at the 1½", 3", 4½", and 6½" points.

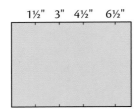

2. Fold and pin the rectangle around the wooden dowel so that the 1½" marks are aligned on the back of the dowel. Sew ⅛" from the edge of the dowel using its straight edge as a guideline as shown. Remove the dowel and press the fold to one side.

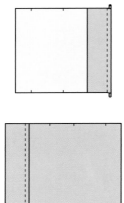

3. Repeat step 2 to sew the remaining folds on the marked rectangle. Press the folds in the same direction after sewing each fold. The finished

block should be 5½" square, including the seam allowances.

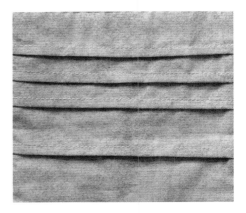

Assembling the Quilt Top

1. Sew a pink striped 2½" x 5½" rectangle to opposite sides of a light blue 5½" square as shown to make a unit. Press the seam allowances toward the light blue square. Repeat to make a total of four units.

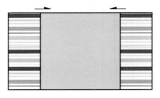

Make 4.

2. Sew a light blue square to opposite sides of a unit from step 1 as shown to make a pieced strip. (Sew the folded-seam unit from step 3 of "Folded Seams" on the right side of one unit from step 1 as shown in the photo on page 30.) Press the seam allowances toward the light blue squares. Make another pieced strip using the last two light blue squares.

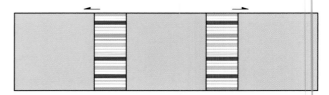

3. Sew the remaining units from step 1 to opposite sides of the Mitered Square block as shown to make a center strip. Press the seam allowances toward the Mitered Square block.

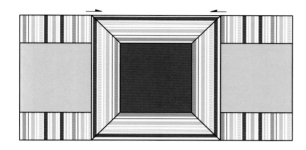

4. Arrange and sew the two pieced strips and the center strip together as shown. Press the seam allowances in one direction.

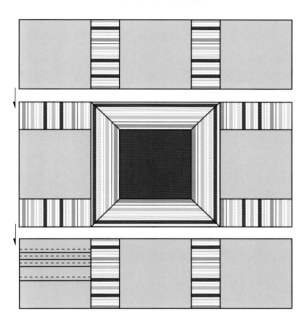

5. Lay one pink striped 2½" x 21½" strip on one side of the quilt center from step 4, right sides together and raw edges aligned as shown. You'll be sewing the strips to the quilt top in a counterclockwise direction using a partial seam. Pin and sew the border strip, leaving about 1" open at one end as shown. Press the seam allowances toward the pink strip.

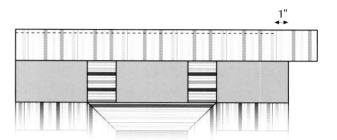

6. Sew a pink striped strip to the left side of the quilt center as shown. Add the remaining pink strips as shown in the quilt assembly diagram on page 39. After the last strip is added, sew the open section of the border seam closed. Press all seam allowances toward the newly added border strips.

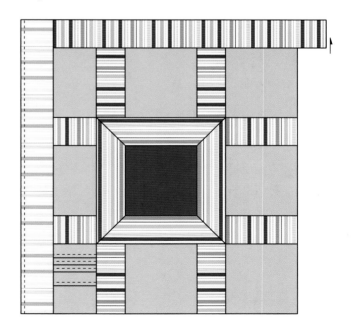

EMBELLISHING THE BLOCKS

Refer to the embellishing techniques on pages 19–22 for detailed instructions as needed. Refer to the photo on page 30 for embellishment placement ideas. For the beads, sequins, and button embellishments, you may want to plan a linear design, but I like the freestyle look in the side squares, with the linear embellishments in the corner squares.

Ruffles

1. To make the ruffles, using the longest stitch length on your sewing machine and cream thread, sew a straight line down the center of each cream floral rectangle. Pulling on one thread, gather the rectangle to a length of 5". Make a total of three ruffles.

2. Pin one ruffle in the center of a light blue square. Pin the remaining ruffles on each side of the first ruffle as shown in the photo below. Topstitch in the center of each ruffle to complete the block.

Tucked or Untucked

You can either leave all four edges of each ruffle exposed, or you can tuck the short ends into the seams, as I did. To do this, gather the ruffles to 5½" (instead of 5") and use a seam ripper to remove enough stitches to make a 1" opening in the seam. Tuck the ends into the seam, and then flip the quilt over and resew the seam.

Beads

1. To add beads, cut a piece of brown thread about 20" long and make a knot at one end. Bring the needle up through the back center of a light blue square and through a pink, brown, or gold bead. Insert the needle down through the fabric close to where it came up. Repeat the process going through the the bead twice to ensure that the bead is secure on the square. In the same manner, group beads by color around the center bead in odd-numbered clusters (1, 3, 5, or 7) by personal preference to complete the block.

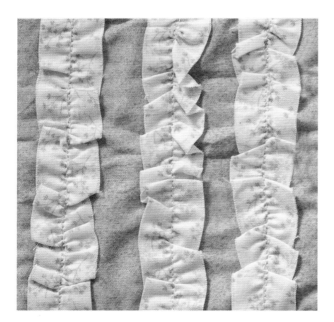

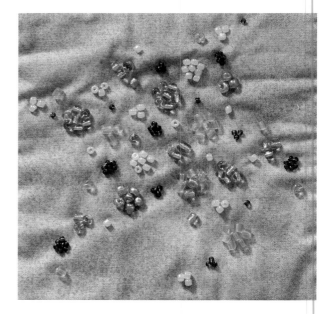

2. If you choose to draw a design with lines of beads rather than clusters, first use a chalk marker to draw the design on the square. You will need to couch the line of beads to the square. To couch a line of beads, bring the needle up through the fabric square and string the number of beads desired on the thread. Before inserting the needle again, make sure that you allow enough space so the beads will lie flat. Insert the needle down through the fabric so the beads are tightly secured by the stitch. Bring the needle up one or two beads from the end of the line and cross over the thread, inserting the needle down on the other side as shown. This secures the line of beads to the fabric square. Depending on the length of the line of beads you'll need to repeat the process every two or three beads to secure them to the fabric square.

Yo-Yos

Referring to "Yo-Yos" on page 21 and using the brown A circles and the pink A circles, make a total of three brown and three pink yo-yos. Referring to the photo above right, place the yo-yos on a light blue square; pin in place. Use matching thread to sew the yo-yos in place to complete the block.

Buttons

To add buttons, cut a piece of cream thread about 20" long and make a knot at one end. Bring the needle up through the back center of a light blue square and through one hole on a cream button. For a four-holed button, insert the needle down through the diagonal hole, bring the needle up through the adjacent hole, and down through the diagonal hole, creating an X. Repeat to secure the button to the fabric square. In the same manner, group the assorted buttons around the center button, sewing them on in the traditional manner to complete the block.

Embroidery

1. To add embroidery stitches, use a chalk marker or water-soluble pen to draw parallel lines ¼" apart in the center of a light blue square. Draw two more parallel lines ¾" apart on each side of the center lines as shown.

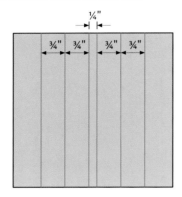

2. Using two strands of blue embroidery floss and the center parallel lines as guidelines, zigzag stitch down the center of the block. Using three strands of yellow embroidery floss and the lines on both sides of the zigzag as guidelines, make a line of coral stitches. Using four strands of pink embroidery floss and the outermost two marked lines as guidelines, make a line of modified chain stitches.

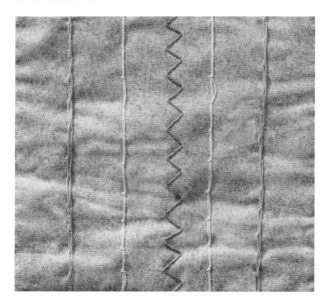

Appliquéd Circles

To make the fusible appliqué circles, remove the paper backing from the brown, cream-and-blue print, cream floral, pink striped, and pink dotted circles. Place the circles on a light blue square as shown in the photo below or in a design of your choice. When you are satisfied with the placement, fuse in place. Using four strands of coordinating embroidery floss, make a ring of split stitches around the edge of each circle.

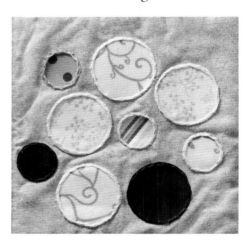

Sequins

1. To add sequins, using metallic silver thread and beginning in the center of a light blue square, bring the needle up in the center of a sequin (A) and back down along the outer edge of the sequin (B). Bring the needle up again through the center and down on the opposite edge (C), creating a straight line across the sequin. In the same manner, group the assorted sequins around the center sequin by personal preference to complete the block. Smaller sequins can be layered on top of larger ones for variety.

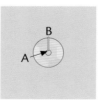
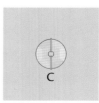

2. If you don't like the look of the silver thread across the sequin, you can use small seed beads in the center of the sequins. Bring the needle up through the sequin and then through a matching seed bead before inserting it back down through the hole of the sequin. The bead will keep the sequin secure on the fabric without any thread showing.

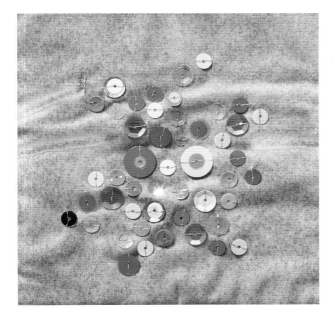

ADDING BORDERS

Referring to "Borders" on page 22, measure, cut, and sew the brown 3½"-wide inner-border strips and the light blue 8½"-wide outer-border strips to the quilt top. Border lengths should be as shown below. Press all seam allowances toward the newly added border strips.

Inner-border strips: 23½" each for sides; 29½" each for top and bottom

Outer-border strips: 29½" each for sides; 45½" each for top and bottom

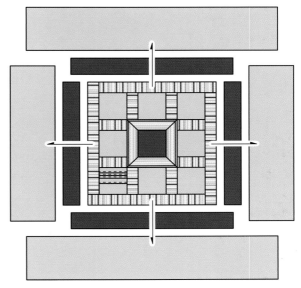

Quilt assembly

EMBELLISHING THE OUTER BORDER

Refer to embellishing techniques on pages 19–22 for detailed instructions as needed. Refer to the photo on page 30 for embellishment placement ideas. Just as in the quilt center, it's possible to change the layout of the embellishments to suit your style. I like the almost symmetric placement of the flowers and vines on opposite corners.

Appliqué Flower

To make the starch-appliqué flower, place one pink striped, two brown, and two pink dotted petals in one corner of the outer border. Position the petals so that one end of each petal is touching in the center of the flower; pin in place. In the same manner, pin the remaining flower petals in the opposite corner as shown in the photo below.

Couched Yarn

1. To couch the gray novelty yarn, cut four 21"-long strands. Referring to the photo on page 41, slip one end of a yarn strand underneath a flower petal. Stitch to secure the end in place. Curve the remainder of the strand in an S shape or a curlicue to coordinate with the curve of the bias strip vine, according to your preference. Pin in place. Cut off any excess yarn.

2. Sew the yarn in place with a couching stitch and gray thread. To make a couching stitch, bring the needle up next to the yarn strand and cross over it, inserting the needle on the other side. Continue the couching stitch the entire length of the strand, spacing the stitches about ½" apart to secure the yarn in place. Repeat to couch all four strands as shown in the quilt photo.

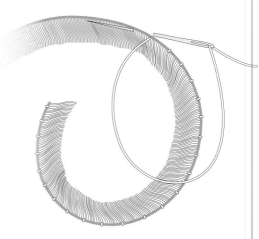

Bias Vines

1. To make the bias-strip vines, fold each cream-and-blue strip in half lengthwise, wrong sides together and raw edges aligned. Sew a scant ¼" from the raw edge.

2. Trim the seam allowance to ⅛". Slide the bias pressing bar inside the fabric tube. Twist the fabric until the seam allowance is centered along one side of the pressing bar. Press the tube flat with the seam allowance open as shown. Remove the pressing bar and press flat again from the right side of the strip. Make a total of four bias strips.

3. Referring to the photo above, slip one end of a bias strip underneath a flower petal. Stitch to secure in place. Curve the remainder of the bias strip in an S shape or a curlicue according to your preference and pin in place.

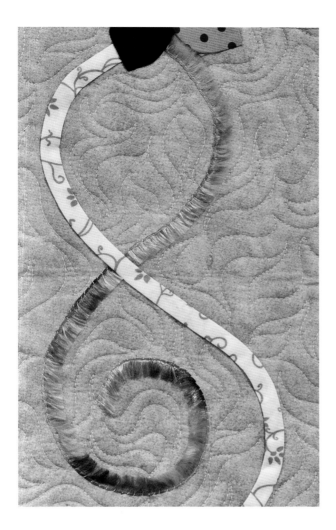

FINISHING

Refer to the finishing techniques on pages 23–25 for detailed instructions if needed.

1. Layer the quilt top, backing, and batting and baste the layers together.

2. Hand or machine quilt as desired.

3. Using the pink striped 2¼"-wide binding strips, prepare the binding and sew it to your quilt.

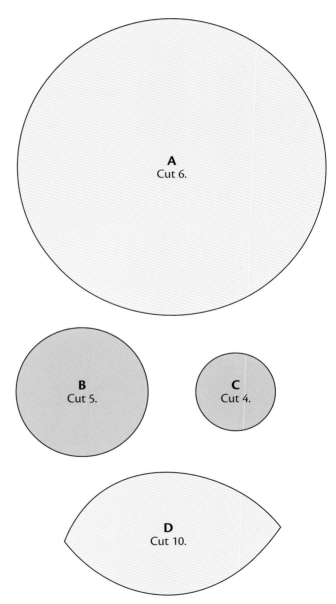

4. Stitch the bias strip in place using an invisible stitch. To make an invisible stitch, bring the needle up underneath the bias strip along the folded edge and through the bottom layer *only*. Slide the needle between the layers of the bias strip for about ½"; then bring it back down through the bias strip and the background fabric. Repeat the stitch along both sides of the bias strip. Fold the end of the strip under to make a clean line at the end and stitch in place. Repeat to stitch two bias strips in opposite corners of the outer border as shown in the photo on page 30.

Stitching the Flower

Hand stitch each flower petal in place using coordinating thread. Sew matching tan buttons in the center of each flower as shown in the photo on page 40.

Cuddle up in comfort with this recycled corduroy throw. Make the woods your own with beads of different sizes and colors.

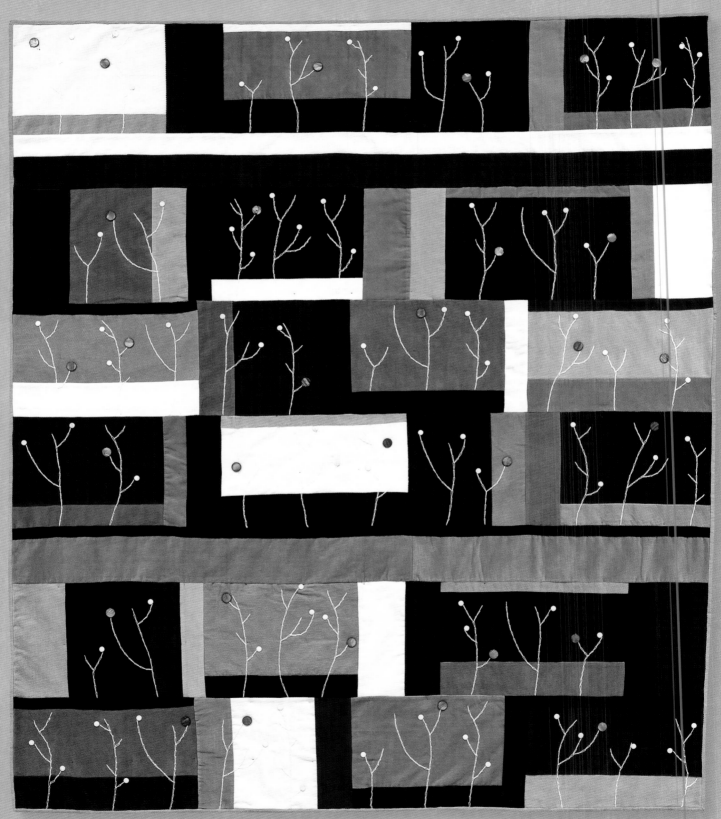

Pieced and tied by Leah Fehr

Finished quilt: 60½" x 70½" • Finished blocks: 10" x 13", 10" x 10", 10" x 16"

Cord of Woods

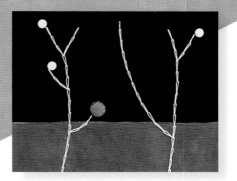

MATERIALS

Yardage is based on 42"-wide fabric.

1 yard of red corduroy for blocks and sashing

1 yard of cream corduroy for blocks and binding

1 yard of off-white corduroy for blocks and sashing

⅞ yard of beige corduroy for blocks and sashing

⅔ yard of tan corduroy for blocks

⅔ yard of black corduroy for blocks and sashing

⅔ yard of eggplant corduroy for blocks

⅔ yard of brown corduroy for blocks

½ yard of gold corduroy for blocks

4¼ yards of fabric for backing

67" x 77" piece of batting

5 skeins of 25 meters (27 yards) per skein, size 5 white pearl cotton thread

110 flat, circular ⅝" brown beads and ⅜" off-white beads

Dressmakers chalk

CUTTING

From the red corduroy, cut:

2 strips, 3½" x 42"

1 rectangle, 8½" x 13½"

1 rectangle, 7½" x 10½"

1 rectangle, 6½" x 16½"

1 rectangle, 5½" x 10½"

2 rectangles, 3½" x 16½"

2 rectangles, 3½" x 10½"

1 rectangle, 2½" x 10½"

1 rectangle, 1½" x 16½"

From the cream corduroy, cut:

8 binding strips, 2¼" x 42"

1 rectangle, 8½" x 13½"

1 rectangle, 3½" x 16½"

1 rectangle, 3½" x 10½"

1 rectangle, 2½" x 13½"

1 rectangle, 1½" x 16½"

From the off-white corduroy, cut:

2 strips, 2½" x 42"

1 rectangle, 8½" x 13½"

1 rectangle, 7½" x 10½"

1 rectangle, 6½" x 16½"

1 rectangle, 5½" x 10½"

1 rectangle, 4½" x 10½"

1 rectangle, 3½" x 16½"

1 rectangle, 3½" x 10½"

1 rectangle, 2½" x 13½"

2 rectangles, 2½" x 10½"

1 rectangle, 1½" x 16½"

From the beige corduroy, cut:

2 strips, 4½" x 42"

1 rectangle, 6½" x 16½"

1 rectangle, 5½" x 10½"

1 rectangle, 4½" x 10½"

1 rectangle, 3½" x 16½"

2 rectangles, 3½" x 10½"

1 rectangle, 2½" x 10½"

1 rectangle, 1½" x 16½"

From the tan corduroy, cut:
1 rectangle, 8½" x 13½"
1 rectangle, 7½" x 10½"
2 rectangles, 6½" x 16½"
1 rectangle, 3½" x 16½"
2 rectangles, 3½" x 10½"
2 rectangles, 2½" x 13½"

From the black corduroy, cut:
2 strips, 1½" x 42"
1 rectangle, 8½" x 13½"
1 rectangle, 7½" x 10½"
1 rectangle, 3½" x 16½"
2 rectangles, 3½" x 10½"
1 rectangle, 2½" x 13½"
1 rectangle, 2½" x 10½"
1 rectangle, 1½" x 16½"

From the eggplant corduroy, cut:
1 rectangle, 8½" x 13½"
1 rectangle, 7½" x 10½"
1 rectangle, 6½" x 16½"
1 rectangle, 5½" x 10½"
2 rectangles, 3½" x 10½"
1 rectangle, 2½" x 13½"
1 rectangle, 2½" x 10½"
1 rectangle, 1½" x 16½"

From the brown corduroy, cut:
1 rectangle, 8½" x 13½"
1 rectangle, 7½" x 10½"
1 rectangle, 6½" x 16½"
1 rectangle, 3½" x 16½"
1 rectangle, 3½" x 10½"
1 rectangle, 2½" x 13½"
1 rectangle, 2½" x 10½"
1 rectangle, 1½" x 16½"

From the gold corduroy, cut:
1 rectangle, 8½" x 13½"
1 rectangle, 6½" x 16½"
1 rectangle, 3½" x 10½"
1 rectangle, 2½" x 13½"
1 rectangle, 2½" x 10½"
1 rectangle, 1½" x 16½"

SELECTING FABRICS

The materials list and cutting instructions call for yardage of corduroy off the bolt. It's also possible to use corduroy pants and/or dresses from the thrift store for this quilt. Just substitute one pair of adult-sized pants for each color listed and you'll have plenty of fabric.

The Stretch Factor

Corduroy tends to bunch up before the needle and stretch as you sew. To counter this tendency, keep your blocks taut by holding onto the bottom edge of the seam being sewn. Don't pull on the seam because that will distort the block—just keep a good grip on the end. Also, wide-wale corduroy stretches more than standard corduroy. If you use some in your quilt, whenever possible, try to have the wide-wale piece on top as you pin and sew the blocks together. Don't use wide-wale corduroy for the binding or in any borders you decide to add to your quilt.

MAKING THE BLOCKS

1. Randomly arrange and sew together one 8½" x 13½" rectangle and one 2½" x 13½" rectangle as shown to make block A. Press the seam allowances to one side. The block should measure 13½" x 10½", including seam allowances. Repeat to make a total of eight A blocks.

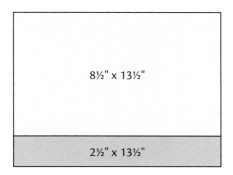

Block A.
Make 8.

> ### Keeping It Plush
>
> To keep the texture intact and not mat down the plush of the corduroy, first lightly press your blocks on the wrong side. Then flip your block over and finger-press the seam allowance on the front of the block. If you're using heavier-weight corduroy, you may want to press the seam allowances open. Also, later when embellishing the blocks, don't use an embroidery hoop or else you will have a long-lasting circle on your blocks when you remove the hoop.

2. Randomly arrange and sew together one 7½" x 10½" rectangle and one 3½" x 10½" rectangle as shown to make block B. Press the seam allowances to one side. The block should measure 10½" x 10½", including seam allowances. Repeat to make a total of six B blocks.

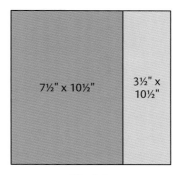

Block B.
Make 6.

3. Randomly arrange and sew together one 3½" x 16½" rectangle, one 6½" x 16½" rectangle, and one 1½" x 16½" rectangle as shown to make block C. Press the seam allowances in one direction. The block should measure 16½" x 10½", including seam allowances. Repeat to make a total of eight C blocks.

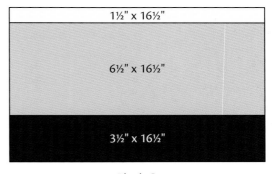

Block C.
Make 8.

EMBELLISHING

1. Using the tree patterns on pages 48 and 49 as a guide and dressmakers chalk, trace tree outlines onto each block. I stitched two trees on each B block and three trees on each of the A and C blocks. Refer to the photo on page 42 as needed. However, you can arrange the trees to your own preferences. You can also draw the trees freehand instead of using the patterns.

2. Refer to "Modified Chain Stitch" on page 22. Using two strands of white pearl cotton and a modified chain stitch, embroider the marked tree patterns onto each block.

3. Sew brown and off-white beads on each tree to represent leaves. I used approximately five beads per block.

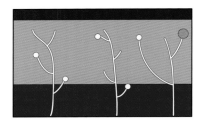

ASSEMBLING THE QUILT TOP

1. Arrange the A, B, and C blocks and the remaining rectangles in rows as shown. Sew the blocks and rectangles together, pressing the seam allowances in one direction. Make two of each row (six total).

2. Measure the length of all six block rows. If they differ, estimate the average and consider this the length. They should measure 60½".

3. Sew the beige 4½"-wide strips together end to end to make a continuous strip. Cut the long strip to fit your measurement from step 2.

4. In the same manner, sew together the red 3½"-wide strips, the off-white 2½"-wide strips, and then the black 1½"-wide strips.

5. Sew the trimmed red strip and off-white strip together along one long edge as shown to make a sashing strip. Press the seam allowances toward the red strip.

6. Sew the trimmed black strip and beige strip together along one long edge as shown to make a sashing strip. Press the seam allowances toward the black strip.

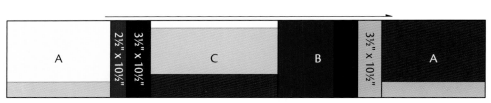

Make 2.

Make 2.

Make 2.

7. Sew the block rows and sashing strips from steps 5 and 6 together as shown in the quilt assembly diagram. Press the seam allowances in one direction.

Finishing

Refer to the finishing techniques on pages 23–25 for detailed instructions if needed.

1. Baste around the quilt top about ⅛" from the outer edge to stabilize the seams, being careful not to stretch the seams as you sew.

2. Layer the quilt top with batting and backing and baste the layers together.

3. Machine quilt or tie as desired.

4. Using the cream 2¼"-wide binding strips, prepare the binding and sew it to your quilt.

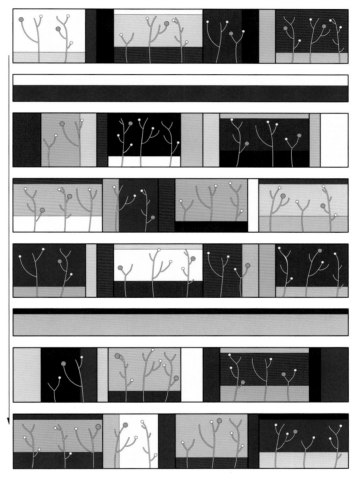

Quilt assembly

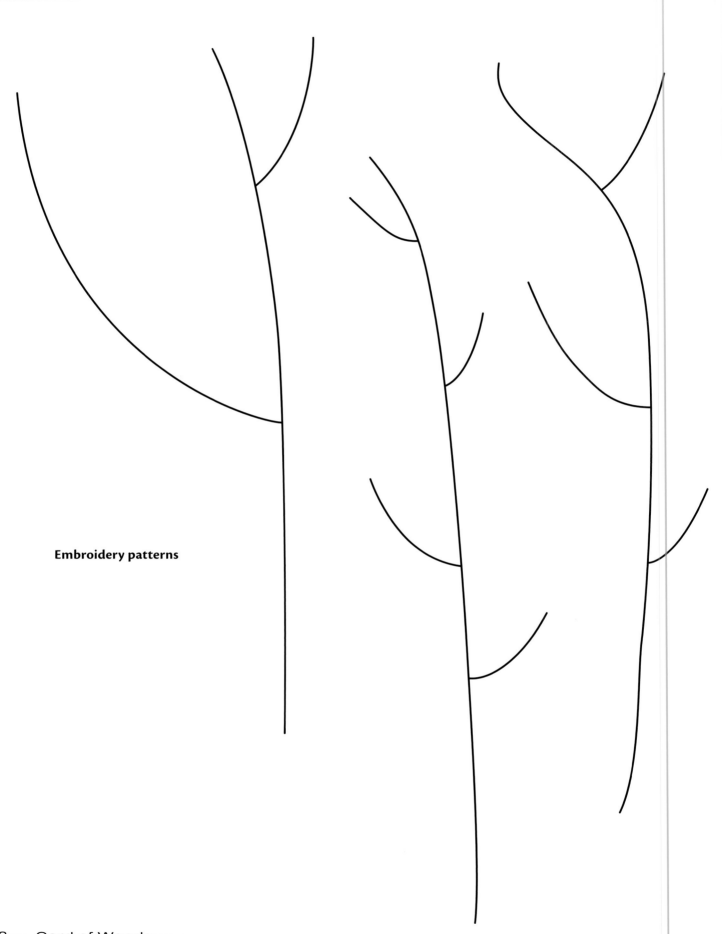

Embroidery patterns

Embroidery patterns

nspired by the boldness of beach accessories and the sparkle of the sea, this graphic throw blends fun and function with its mitered corners and colorful sequins.

Pieced by Leah Fehr and machine quilted by Penny Miller

Finished quilt: 47½" x 58½" • Finished blocks: 10" x 10"

Summer Stripes

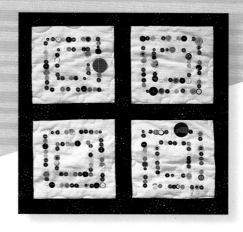

MATERIALS

Yardage is based on 42"-wide fabric.

1¾ yards of white solid for blocks

1½ yards of black print for sashing, border, and binding

⅔ yard of pink-and-black striped fabric for blocks

½ yard of black dotted fabric for blocks

3¼ yards of fabric for backing

54" x 65" piece of batting

Assorted sizes of pink, clear, black, red, white, and gold sequins

Metallic silver thread

Pencil or chalk marker

Water-soluble pen

CUTTING

From the white solid, cut:

29 strips, 1½" x 42"; crosscut into;

- 32 rectangles, 1½" x 10½"
- 32 rectangles, 1½" x 8½"
- 32 rectangles, 1½" x 6½"
- 32 rectangles, 1½" x 4½"

16 squares, 5" x 5"

16 squares, 2½" x 2½"

From the *lengthwise grain* of the pink-and-black striped fabric, cut:

32 rectangles, 1½" x 8½"

32 rectangles, 1½" x 4½"

From the black dotted fabric, cut:

10 strips, 1½" x 42"; crosscut into:

- 16 rectangles, 1½" x 8½"
- 16 rectangles, 1½" x 6½"
- 16 rectangles, 1½" x 4½"
- 16 rectangles, 1½" x 2½"

From the black print, cut:

6 border strips, 2½" x 42"

6 binding strips, 2¼" x 42"

13 strips, 1½" x 42"; crosscut *8 of the strips* into:

- 19 rectangles, 1½" x 10½"
- 8 rectangles, 1½" x 5"

MAKING BLOCK A

1. On the wrong side of eight white 2½" squares, use a pencil or chalk marker to mark each corner ¼" from the raw edge as shown in preparation for making mitered corners.

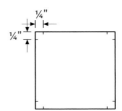

2. Fold each marked white square in half, right sides together, vertically and horizontally. Finger-press to mark the center of each side as shown.

3. Fold each pink-and-black 1½" x 4½" rectangle in half, wrong sides together. Finger-press one side to mark the center as shown.

4. With right sides together, place a marked white square on a creased rectangle, matching the center creases as shown; pin in place. Pin a rectangle on the opposite side of the square in the same manner.

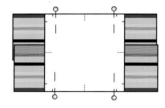

5. With the white square on top, sew the rectangles to the white square, starting and stopping at the ¼" marks with a small backstitch. Press the seam allowances toward the white square.

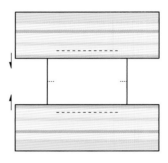

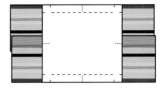

6. Repeat steps 4 and 5 to sew rectangles to the remaining sides of the white square. The unstitched ends of the rectangle will extend beyond the square.

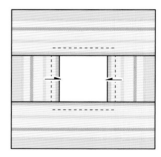

7. Fold the white square in half diagonally, right sides together, and align the edges of the rectangles as shown. Draw a diagonal line from the corner of the rectangle to the seam line. Stitch exactly on the marked line, sewing from the inner corner to the outer edge to make a mitered corner. Trim the seam allowance to ¼" and press the seam allowances to one side.

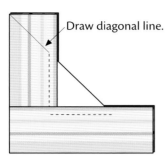

Draw diagonal line.

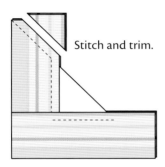

Stitch and trim.

8. Miter the remaining corners in the same manner. Make a total of eight units, each measuring 4½" square.

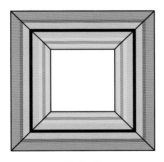

Make 8.

Don't Skimp

To ensure your blocks turn out the correct size, take your time with each one. After adding each round of strips, measure your block to be certain it's the size specified in the instructions. If not, rip out the seams and start again. Take your time and measure, measure, measure.

9. Sew white 1½" x 4½" rectangles to opposite sides of each mitered square. Sew white 1½" x 6½" rectangles to the remaining sides as shown. Press all seam allowances toward the striped fabric. Make eight units, each measuring 6½" square.

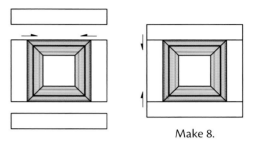

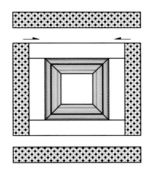

Make 8.

10. Sew black dotted 1½" x 6½" rectangles to opposite sides of each unit from step 9. Sew black dotted 1½" x 8½" rectangles to the remaining sides of the unit. Press all seam allowances toward the black dotted rectangles. Make eight units, each measuring 8½" square.

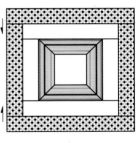

Make 8.

11. Sew white 1½" x 8½" rectangles to opposite edges of the unit from step 10. Sew white 1½" x 10½" rectangles to the remaining sides of the unit. Press all seam allowances toward the black dotted rectangles to complete block A. Make a total of eight A blocks, each measuring 10½" square, including seam allowances.

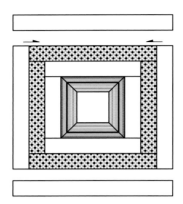

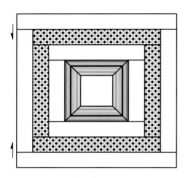

Make 8.

MAKING BLOCK B

1. Sew black dotted 1½" x 2½" rectangles to opposite sides of each remaining white 2½" square. Sew black dotted 1½" x 4½" rectangles to the remaining sides of each square as shown. Press all seam allowances toward the black dotted rectangles. Make eight units, each measuring 4½" square.

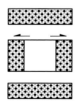

Make 8.

2. Sew white 1½" x 4½" rectangles to opposite sides of each unit from step 1. Sew white 1½" x 6½" rectangles to the remaining sides of each unit. Press all seam allowances toward the black dotted rectangles. Make eight units, each measuring 6½" square.

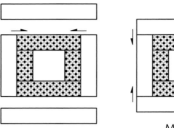

Make 8.

3. In the same manner as block A, steps 1–7, sew four pink-and-black striped 1½" x 8½" rectangles to the unit, mitering the corners as shown. Press the seam allowances toward the white rectangles. Make eight units, each measuring 8½" square.

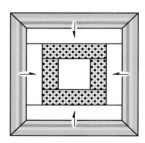

4. Sew white 1½" x 8½" rectangles to opposite sides of each mitered unit. Sew white 1½" x 10½" rectangles to the remaining sides of each unit. Press all seam allowances toward the striped rectangles to complete block B. Make a total of eight B blocks, each measuring 10½" square, including seam allowances.

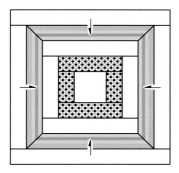

Make 8.

Making Block C

1. Sew white 5" squares to opposite long edges of each black 1½" x 5" rectangle to make a half-block unit as shown. Press the seam allowances toward the black rectangle. Make a total of eight units.

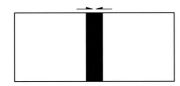

Make 8.

2. Sew together two half-block units and one black 1½" x 10½" rectangle as shown to make block C. Press the seam allowances toward the black rectangle. Make four C blocks, each measuring 10½" square, including seam allowances.

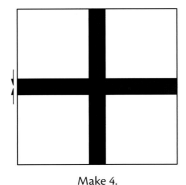

Make 4.

Embellishing

1. To embellish the C blocks, use a water-soluble pen to draw a small square inside a larger square in each white square as shown.

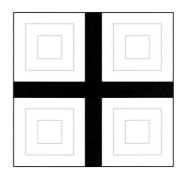

2. Layer and sew the assorted sequins to the white squares using the marked lines as a guide. Using metallic silver thread, bring the needle up in the center of a sequin and back down along the sequin's edge. Bring the needle up again through the center, and down on the opposite edge, creating a straight line across the sequin. Smaller sequins can be layered on top of larger ones for variety. You can also use small seed beads in the center of the sequins; bring the needle up through the one or two sequins and then through a seed bead before inserting it down again through the center hole of the sequin.

Assembling the Quilt Top

1. Arrange and sew the blocks and remaining black 1½" x 10½" rectangles in five rows, alternating them as shown in the assembly diagram below. Press the seam allowances toward the black rectangles.

2. Measure the length of the block rows; they should measure 43½". If they differ, calculate the average and consider this the length. Sew together the black 1½"-wide strips end to end to make a long strip: From this strip, cut four sashing strips the length of your row measurement.

3. Sew together the block rows and four sashing strips from step 2, alternating them as shown in the assembly diagram. Press the seam allowances toward the sashing strips. The quilt top should measure 43½" x 54½", including seam allowances.

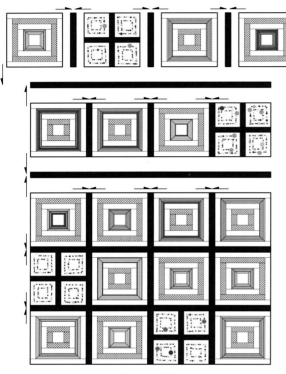

Quilt assembly

4. Referring to "Borders" on page 22, measure, cut, and sew the black 2½"-wide border strips to the quilt top. The border strips should be 54½" each for sides; 47½" each for top and bottom. Press all seam allowances toward the newly added border strips.

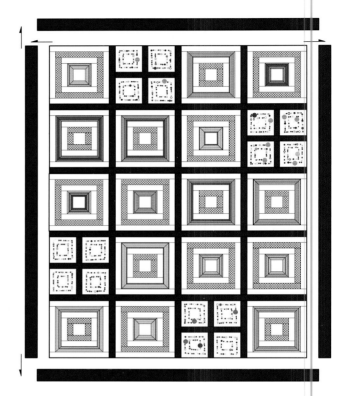

Finishing

Refer to the finishing techniques on pages 23–25 for detailed instructions if needed.

1. Layer the quilt top, backing, and batting and baste the layers together.

2. Hand or machine quilt as desired.

3. Using the black 2¼"-wide binding strips, prepare the binding and sew it to your quilt.

Casual Friday

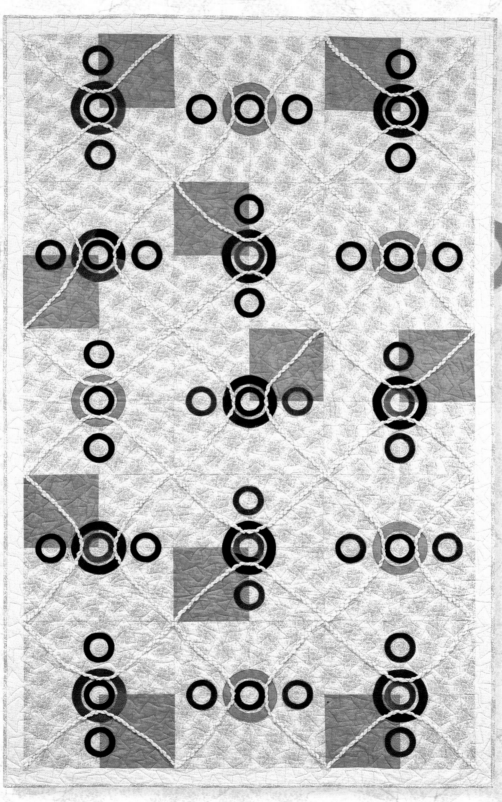

Pieced by Leah Fehr and machine quilted by Penny Miller

Finished quilt: 52" x 84" • Finished block: 16" x 16"

Chunky yarn and worn denim combine to make any day relaxed with this calming, twin-size quilt.

MATERIALS

Yardage is based on 42"-wide fabric.

4 yards of light print for blocks and binding

1 yard of mottled green fabric for blocks and circle appliqués

1 yard of dark blue fabric or recycled denim for circle appliqués

⅝ yard of cream print for border

5½ yards of fabric for backing

58" x 90" piece of batting

⅔ yard of 16"-wide fusible web

5 skeins of 25m (27 yards) per skein, size 5 khaki pearl cotton

1 skein or 160 yds of off-white bulky (chunky weight 5) acrylic yarn for embellishing★

Orange variegated thread

★*If you'd rather not cut and braid all those lengths of yarns, you can use single lengths of a chunkier yarn. You'll need 27 yds.*

SELECTING FABRICS

The instructions call for dark blue fabric for the appliqué circles. The quilt shown was made with denim from thrift-store jeans. Three pairs should yield enough for the circles; however, to have a larger variety of colors, use up to six pairs.

PREPARING FUSIBLE APPLIQUÉS

Referring to "Fusible Appliqué" on page 18 and using the patterns on page 61, trace 15 large circles and 45 small circles onto the paper side of fusible web. Group the circles together on the fusible web so you can fuse them as a single unit to the wrong side of the fabrics. Fuse 5 large circles onto the mottled green fabric, 10 large circles and 45 small circles onto the dark blue or recycled denim fabric.

CUTTING

From the light print, cut:
8 binding strips, 2¼" x 42"
50 squares, 8½" x 8½"

From the mottled green fabric, cut:
10 squares, 8½" x 8½"
5 large circles, prepared with fusible web

From the dark blue fabric or recycled denim, cut:
10 large circles, prepared with fusible web
45 small circles, prepared with fusible web

From the cream print, cut:
7 border strips, 2¼" x 42"

MAKING THE BLOCKS

1. Arrange three light print squares and one mottled green square in two rows as shown. Sew the squares together into rows. Press the seam allowances to one side, alternating the direction from one row to the next. Sew the rows together to complete a green Four Patch block. Press the seam allowances in one direction. Make a total of 10 green Four Patch blocks.

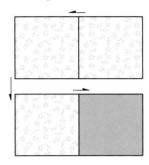

Make 10.

2. Arrange and sew four light print squares together into rows in the same manner as the green Four Patch blocks. Make a total of five light Four Patch blocks.

APPLIQUÉING THE CIRCLES

1. Remove the paper backing from one blue large and three blue small circles. Referring to the quilt assembly diagram on page 60 for placement guidance, place the circles on a green Four Patch block as shown. When you are satisfied with the placement, fuse in place. Using one strand of the khaki pearl cotton, make a ring of split stitches around the edge of each circle. Refer to "Split Stitch" on page 22 as needed for details. Repeat for all 10 green Four Patch blocks.

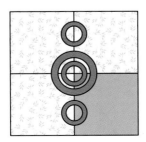

2. In the same manner, appliqué one mottled green large circle and three blue small circles onto a light Four Patch block. Repeat for all five light Four Patch blocks.

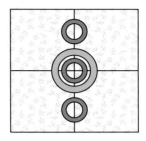

Make 5.

EMBELLISHING

1. Cut 180 pieces of off-white yarn each 32" long.

2. Knot three pieces of yarn together at one end and braid. When finished braiding; knot the end. Repeat to make a total of 60 braids.

3. Twist two braids together to make a double braid. Knot both ends. Repeat to make a total of 30 double braids.

Alternative Embellishments

For a different look, use rickrack or ribbon instead of yarn to embellish your blocks.

4. Fold the double braid in half to find the center, pin a braid on one side of a center small circle. Align the center of the braid with the seam line, and place the ends of the braid in adjacent corners of the block as shown. When you are satisfied with the placement, use orange variegated thread to cross-stitch the braid in place. In the same manner, sew a double braid onto the opposite side of the block. Repeat to embellish all 15 appliquéd blocks.

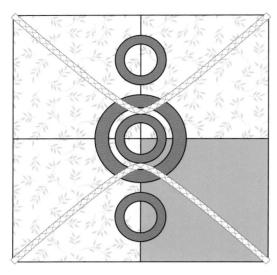

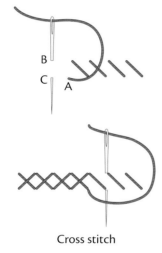

Cross stitch

ASSEMBLING THE QUILT TOP

1. Arrange the blocks in five rows of three blocks each as shown in the quilt assembly diagram. Sew the blocks together in rows. Press the seam allowances in opposite directions from one row to the next. Then sew the rows together and press the seam allowances in one direction.

2. Referring to "Borders" on page 22, measure, cut, and sew the cream 2¼"-wide border strips to the quilt top. The border strips should be 80½" each for sides; 52" each for top and bottom. Press all seam allowances toward the quilt center.

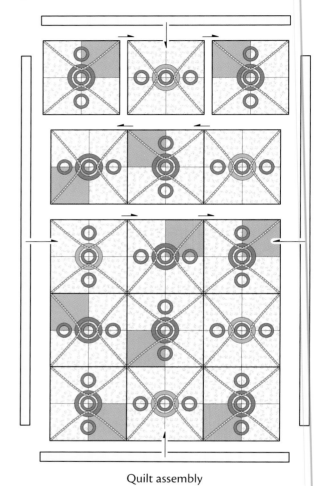

Quilt assembly

FINISHING

Refer to the finishing techniques on pages 23–25 for detailed instructions if needed.

1. Layer the quilt top, backing, and batting and baste the layers together.

2. Hand or machine quilt as desired.

3. Using the light print 2¼"-wide binding strips, prepare the binding and sew it to your quilt.

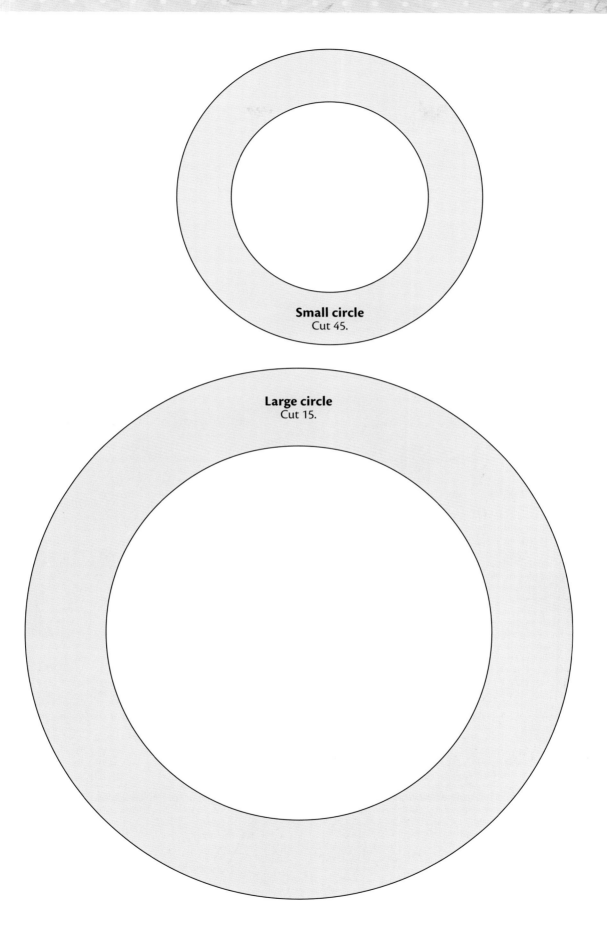

Small circle
Cut 45.

Large circle
Cut 15.

Fabulously feminine ruffles enhance the romantic feel of this throw designed for a chick-flick night on the couch.

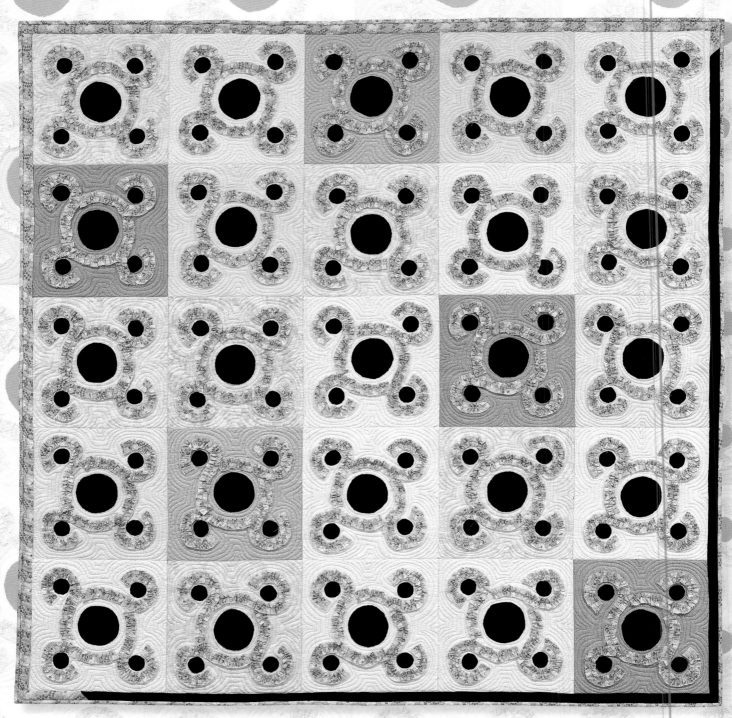

Pieced by Leah Fehr and machine quilted by Penny Miller

Finished quilt: 62½" x 62½" • Finished block: 12" x 12"

Whirlwind Romance

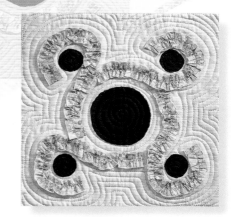

MATERIALS

Yardage is based on 42"-wide fabric.

3½ yards *total* of assorted cream and/or tan prints for blocks

2¼ yards of pink print for embellishments, border, and binding

1 yard of brown solid for appliqués and border

4⅛ yards of fabric for backing

69" x 69" piece of batting

Brown and pink thread

Heat-resistant template plastic

PREPARING STARCH APPLIQUÉS

Referring to "Starch Appliqué" on page 19 and using the large and small circle patterns on page 65, prepare 25 large brown circles and 100 small brown circles. This quilt was made with a starched appliqué method; however, if you prefer, you can use the "Fusible Appliqué" method described on page 18. You'll need 1⅝ yards of 16"-wide fusible web. Group the circles together on the fusible web so you can fuse them as a single unit to the wrong side of the brown fabric.

CUTTING

From the assorted cream and/or tan prints, cut:

25 squares, 12½" x 12½"

From the pink print, cut:

7 binding strips, 2¼" x 42"

4 border strips, 1½" x 42"

100 strips, 1" x 21"

From the brown solid, cut:

3 border strips, 1½" x 42"

25 large circles, prepared for starch appliqué

100 small circles, prepared for starch appliqué

MAKING THE BLOCKS

1. Fold each cream and/or tan square in half diagonally in both directions and finger-press, to create an X across the square. Pin a large brown circle in the center of the X. Pin a small brown circle 2" from the edge of the large circle on each diagonal line as shown.

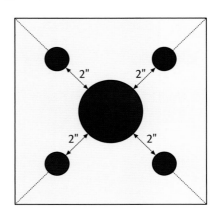

2. Blind hem stitch around each large and small circle with brown thread. To make a blind hem stitch, stitch so that the straight stitches are in the background fabric, very close to the appliqué edge, and the swing stitch is in the appliqué piece. Repeat to make a total of 25 appliquéd blocks.

Blind hem stitch

Keep inside the Line

If you're not as comfortable machine appliquéing as you'd like to be, sew all of the large circles first. By repeating the motion 25 times, you'll be more ready to tackle the small circles. Remember to start stitching with the needle right next to the edge of the circle and use your hands to guide the square under the presser foot, keeping the straight stitch next to the edge of the circle. Go as slowly as you need to. You may need to manually move the needle down into the fabric and pivot the square to regain the placement of your needle next to the edge of the circle. Always remember to put the needle down into the fabric before you lift the presser foot.

Embellishing

Refer to "Ruffles" on page 20 as needed for details.

1. Using the longest stitch length on your sewing machine and pink thread, sew a straight line down the center of each pink 1" x 21" strip. Pulling on one thread, gather the strip to a length of 12". Make a total of 100 ruffles.

2. Pin four ruffles onto an appliquéd block as shown. Topstitch in the center of each ruffle with pink thread to complete the block. Repeat for all 25 appliquéd blocks.

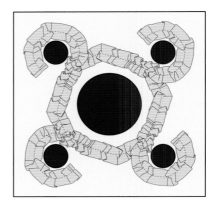

Make 25.

Assembling the Quilt Top

1. Arrange the blocks in five rows of five blocks each as shown in the quilt assembly diagram. Sew the blocks together in rows. Press the seam allowances in opposite directions from one row to the next. Then sew the rows together and press the seam allowances in one direction. The quilt top should measure 60½" x 60½", including seam allowances.

2. Referring to "Borders" on page 22, sew the pink 1½"-wide border strips together end to end. Sew together the brown border strips end to end. Then sew together the long pink strip and the long brown strip end to end to make a continuous strip. Press all seam allowances open.

3. Referring to the photo on page 62 and the quilt assembly diagram, cut the long pink-and-brown strip to make:

- one long border strip, 62½" long
- two medium border strips, 61½" long
- one short border strip, 60½" long

4. Sew the short border strip to one side of the quilt top. Sew the remaining border strips to the quilt top in a clockwise direction, starting with the medium strips and sewing the long border strip last. Press all seam allowances toward the newly added border strips.

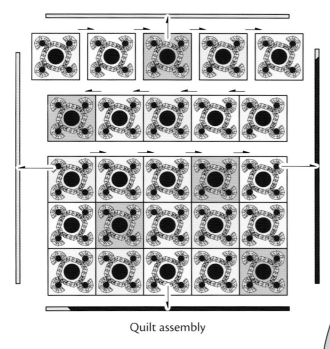

Quilt assembly

FINISHING

Refer to the finishing techniques on pages 23–25 for detailed instructions if needed.

1. Layer the quilt top, backing, and batting and baste the layers together.

2. Hand or machine quilt as desired.

3. Using the pink 2¼"-wide binding strips, prepare the binding and sew it to your quilt.

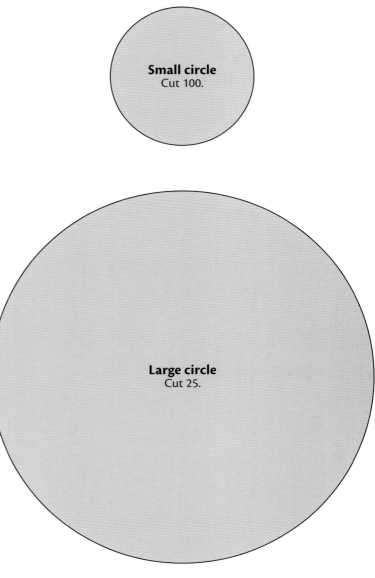

Small circle
Cut 100.

Large circle
Cut 25.

The coral-like arrangement of antique buttons on this wall hanging will transport your decor under the sea.

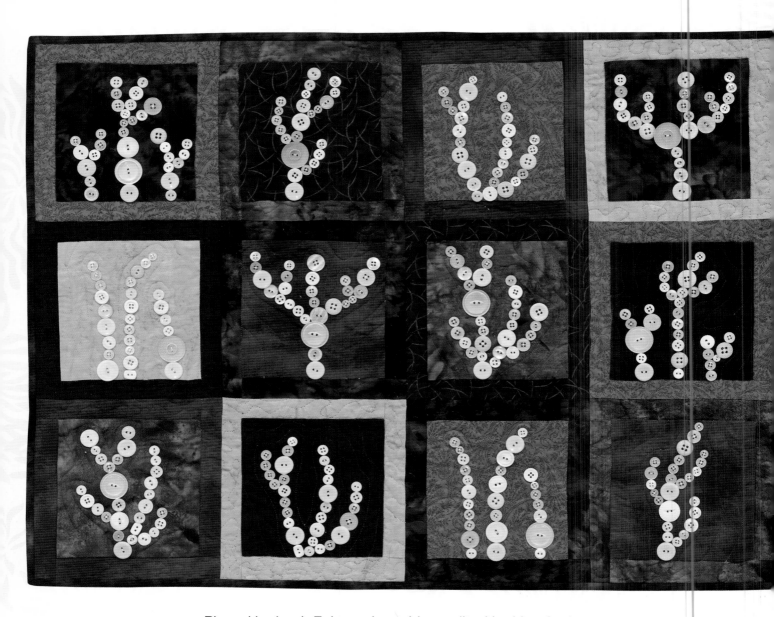

Pieced by Leah Fehr and machine quilted by Lisa Anderson

Finished quilt: 32½" x 24½" • Finished block: 8" x 8"

Sea Buttons

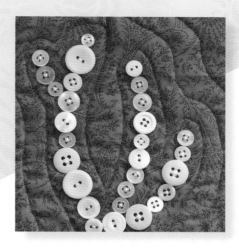

MATERIALS

Yardage is based on 42"-wide fabric.

¼ yard *each* of assorted brown, light green, green, dark green, teal, bright blue, and navy prints and/or batiks for blocks

⅓ yard of dark blue batik for binding

1 yard of fabric for backing

39" x 31" piece of batting

White thread

360 (approximately) small, medium, and large white and off-white buttons

Water-soluble pen or chalk marker

CUTTING

From the assorted prints and/or batiks, cut *a total of:*

12 squares, 6½" x 6½"

48 strips, 1½" x 7½", in matching sets of four

From the dark blue batik, cut:

4 binding strips, 2¼" x 42"

Color Placement

When I cut fabric for this quilt, I cut two squares and two sets of strips from each print or batik. This gave me two extra squares and sets of strips. I arranged all the pieces of the quilt on a table before I sewed them, substituting the extras into the quilt layout until I was pleased with the placement. Even if you don't cut any extra pieces, I still recommend laying out the pieces before you sew any blocks together to get the best color placement for you.

MAKING THE BRIGHT HOPES BLOCKS

1. With right sides together, align one edge of a print or batik strip with a print or batik square as shown. Beginning at the aligned edge, sew the rectangle to the square with a partial seam, stopping about 1" from the square's edge. Press the seam allowance toward the strip.

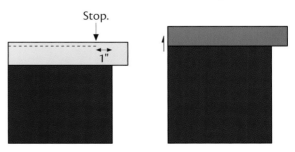

2. Sew a matching print or batik strip to the left side of the square as shown. Press the seam allowance toward the strip. Continue sewing matching strips around the square in the same manner. Complete the partial seam stitched in step 1; press. Make a total of 12 Bright Hopes blocks.

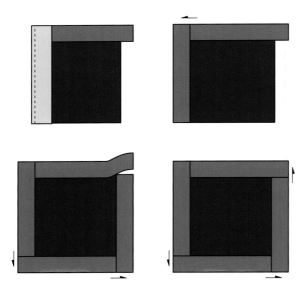

EMBELLISHING

1. Using a light box or other light source and the patterns on pages 69–71, trace a coral pattern on each Bright Hopes block using a water-soluble pen or chalk marker. In the quilt shown, each coral pattern is used twice. Refer to the photo on page 66 for placement ideas.

2. Using white thread, sew buttons to each coral shape beginning at the bottom of the coral and working toward the top and along the branches.

Button Placement
To make the most of your buttons, trace two copies (12 total) of each coral pattern onto scratch paper. Arrange the buttons on each coral shape, adjusting the sizes and colors of the buttons until you are pleased with the results. Leave the buttons on the pieces of paper until you are ready to sew them to the blocks.

ASSEMBLING THE QUILT TOP

1. Arrange the Bright Hopes blocks in three rows of four blocks each as shown in the quilt assembly diagram. Sew the blocks together into rows. Press the seam allowances in opposite directions from one row to the next.

2. Sew the rows together. Press the seam allowances in one direction.

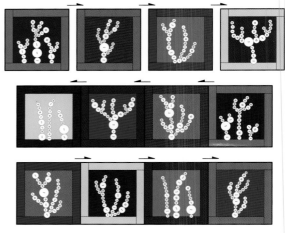

Quilt assembly

FINISHING

Refer to the finishing techniques on pages 23–25 for detailed instructions if needed.

1. Layer the quilt top, backing, and batting and baste the layers together.

2. Hand or machine quilt as desired.

3. Using the dark blue batik 2¼"-wide binding strips, prepare the binding and sew it to your quilt.

Coral patterns

Coral patterns

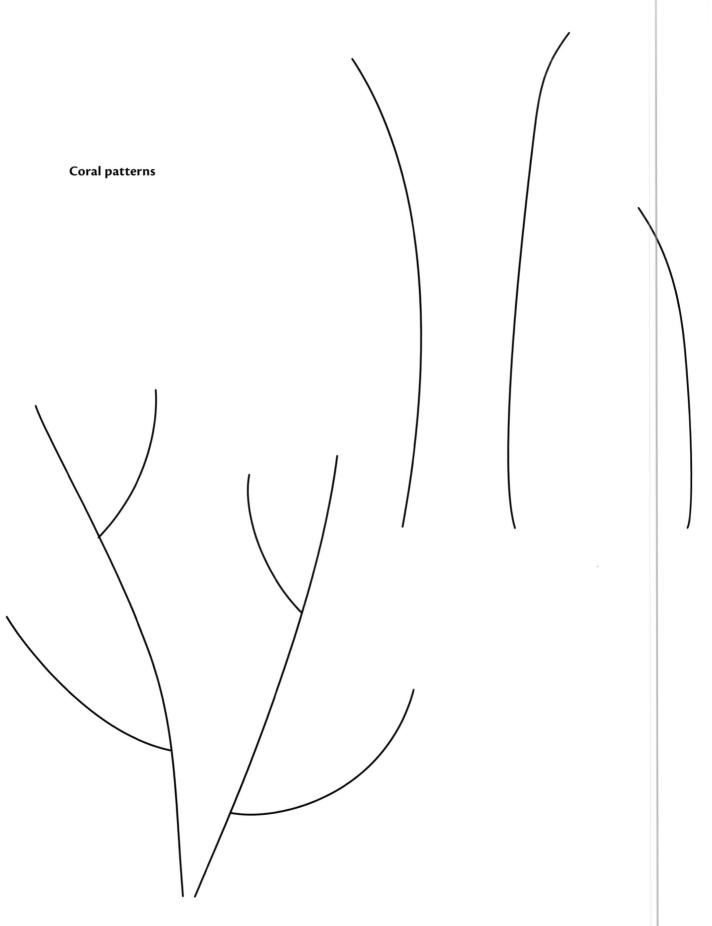

Coral pattern

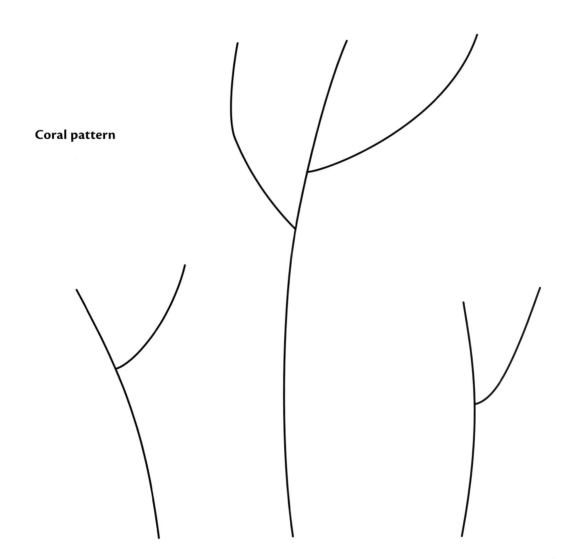

R ecreate the bright and boisterous atmosphere of the circus
with this colorful twin-size quilt perfect for a bunk bed.

Pieced by Leah Fehr and machine quilted by Penny Miller
Finished quilt: 52½" x 76½"

Center Ring

MATERIALS

Yardage is based on 42"-wide fabric.

2⅛ yards of yellow print for blocks, yo-yos, border, and binding

1⅜ yards of brown print for blocks and yo-yos

1⅜ yards of blue batik for blocks and yo-yos

1¼ yards of blue dotted fabric for blocks and yo-yos

1⅛ yards of white solid for blocks and yo-yos

1 yard of red batik for blocks and yo-yos

5 yards of fabric for backing

59" x 83" piece of batting

Yellow, brown, blue, white, and red thread

Marking pen

⅛" wooden dowel

CUTTING

From the white solid, cut:

4 strips, 6½" x 42"; crosscut into 16 rectangles, 6½" x 9"

From the yellow print, cut:

3 strips, 6½" x 42"; crosscut into:
- 7 rectangles, 6½" x 12½"
- 1 square, 6½" x 6½"

7 border strips, 2½" x 42"

7 binding strips, 2¼" x 42"

From the brown print, cut:

3 strips, 6½" x 42"; crosscut into:
- 8 rectangles, 6½" x 12½"
- 1 square, 6½" x 6½"

From the blue batik, cut:

3 strips, 6½" x 42"; crosscut into:
- 7 rectangles, 6½" x 12½"
- 2 squares, 6½" x 6½"

From the blue dotted fabric, cut:

3 strips, 6½" x 42"; crosscut into:
- 7 rectangles, 6½" x 12½"
- 2 squares, 6½" x 6½"

From the red batik, cut:

3 strips, 6½" x 42"; crosscut into:
- 7 rectangles, 6½" x 12½"
- 2 squares, 6½" x 6½"

MAKING THE FOLDED SEAM BLOCKS

Refer to "Folded Seams" on page 19 for detailed instructions.

1. On the right side of eight white rectangles, place marks on each long side at the 1½", 2½", 4", 5½", and 6½" points. On the remaining white rectangles, mark each long side at the 1½", 2½", 4½", 6½", and 7½" points.

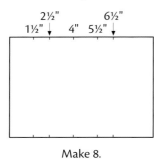

Make 8.

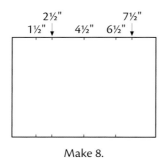

Make 8.

> **Rule of Half**
>
> In the quilt shown each square has five sewn folds. You can sew as many folds, or as few, as you like. To determine the size of rectangle to cut, add ½" for each sewn fold. For example, for the squares in the quilt, I added 2½" (5 x ½") to one side of a 6½" square and cut 6½" x 9" rectangles.

2. Using a wooden dowel, fold and pin the rectangle around the dowel so that the 1½" marks are aligned on the back of the dowel. Sew ⅛" from the edge of the dowel using its straight edge as a guideline as shown. Remove the dowel and press the fold to one side.

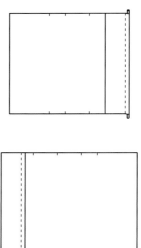

3. Repeat step 2 to sew the remaining folds on each marked rectangle. Press the folds in the same direction after sewing each fold. Each Folded Seam block should be 6½" square, including the seam allowances.

ASSEMBLING THE QUILT TOP

1. Referring to the quilt assembly diagram, lay out the white Folded Seam blocks and the yellow, brown, blue batik, blue dotted, and red batik rectangles and squares in six rows as shown.

2. Sew the pieces together into rows. Press the seam allowances in opposite directions from row to row. Sew the rows together and press the seam allowances in one direction. The quilt top should measure 48½" x 72½", including seam allowances.

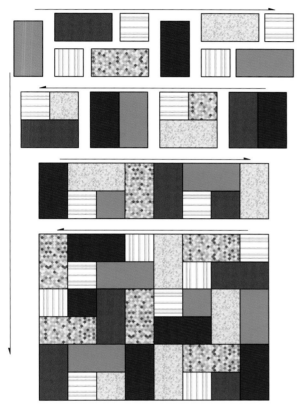

Quilt assembly

Adding the Borders

Referring to "Borders" on page 22, measure, cut, and sew the yellow 2½"-wide border strips to the quilt top. The border strips should be 72½" each for sides; 52½" each for top and bottom. Press all seam allowances toward the newly added border strips.

Embellishing

Refer to "Yo-Yos" on page 21 and "Making Templates" on page 17 as needed for detailed instructions.

1. Use the pattern on page 76 to make 144 yo-yos.
- Make 24 yellow yo-yos
- Make 32 brown yo-yos
- Make 32 blue batik yo-yos
- Make 24 blue dotted yo-yos
- Make 24 white yo-yos
- Make 8 red batik yo-yos

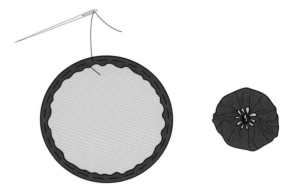

2. Referring to the photo on page 72, place eight matching yo-yos in three diagonal rows on a rectangle. Pin and sew the yo-yos in place with coordinating thread. Repeat to sew yo-yos onto a total of 18 rectangles as shown in the photo.

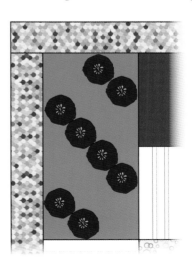

Finishing

Refer to the finishing techniques on pages 23–25 for detailed instructions if needed.

1. Layer the quilt top, backing, and batting and baste the layers together.

2. Hand or machine quilt as desired.

3. Using the yellow 2¼"-wide binding strips, prepare the binding and sew it to your quilt.

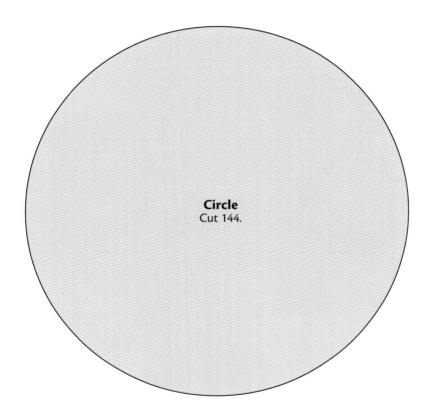

Circle
Cut 144.

Tie Burst

Pieced by Leah Fehr and machine quilted by Lisa Anderson
Finished quilt: 30½" x 36½" • Finished block: 6" x 6"

Uncle Ed's ties never looked so good! Multiple patterns, stripes, and colors blend together to create a wall hanging worthy to be the focal point of any room.

MATERIALS

Yardage is based on 42"-wide fabric.

48 silk or polyester ties *or* 2⅝ yards *total* of assorted stripes and prints for blocks

3 gray and navy silk *or* polyester ties or ⅓ yard of assorted stripes and prints for binding

1⅓ yards of fabric for backing★

36" x 42" piece of batting

2 yards of 22"-wide tear-away stabilizer

¼" bias pressing bar

★If backing fabric is 42" wide after washing, you can use a single width of 1 yard.

SELECTING AND CUTTING THE TIES

The quilt shown was made with silk and polyester men's ties from the 1970s. Most of these ties were extra wide in the front, so I had several strips left over after making the blocks. The number of ties called for in the materials list should give you plenty of fabric and variety in the quilt.

Strip out the entire tie lining material and press the remaining silk (or polyester) flat using a silk setting on the iron. I cut each tie on the seams, yielding two or three pieces, depending on the number of seams, as shown.

From the largest piece, I cut one 1½"-wide strip and one 2"-wide strip. From the remaining part of the large piece, I cut either one 2½"-wide strip or two 1½"-wide strips. From the small middle piece, I cut one 2½"-wide strip. From the medium piece, I cut two 1½"-wide strips. From the gray and navy ties for the binding, I only cut 2¼"-wide strips.

CUTTING

From the assorted stripes and prints, cut:

7 strips, 2½" x 42"

16 strips, 2" x 42"

25 strips, 1½" x 42"★

★Refer to "Smaller Seam Allowances" at right. If you choose to cut 1¼"-wide strips; you'll need 10 strips, 1¼" x 42" and 15 strips, 1½" x 42".

From the gray and navy stripes and prints, cut:

4 binding strips, 2¼" x 42"

From the stabilizer, cut:

30 squares, 6½" x 6½"

PREPARING "BIAS" STRIPS

Because the strips in this quilt will be used to make straight lines, it's okay to cut the bias strips on the straight grain, across the width of fabric (selvage to selvage). If you were going to shape the strips into any kind of curve, you'd need to cut your fabric on the bias.

1. Fold a 1½"-wide strip in half lengthwise, wrong sides together and raw edges aligned. Sew a scant ¼" from the raw edge.

¼"

2. Trim the seam allowance to ⅛". Slide the pressing bar inside the fabric tube. Twist the fabric until the seam allowance is centered along one side of the pressing bar. Press the tube flat with the seam allowance open as shown. Remove the pressing bar and press flat again from the right side of the strip. Make a total of 10 strips totalling about 400".

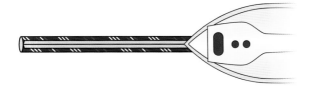

Smaller Seam Allowances

If you're confident in your sewing skills, it's possible to cut your "bias" strips 1¼" wide (rather than 1½" wide) and use a ⅛" seam allowance. This way you don't have to add the extra step of trimming the seam allowances, as in step 2.

MAKING THE BLOCKS

1. Adjust the stitch length on your machine to make a slightly longer stitch so it's easier to remove the stabilizer when the block is finished.

2. Lay one assorted striped or print strip of any width, diagonally, right side up, in the center of one square of stabilizer. Trim the strip end even with the corner of the stabilizer square. Lay a second strip (of any width) right side down on the first strip, with the raw edges on one side aligned as shown. Trim its end even with the end of the first strip.

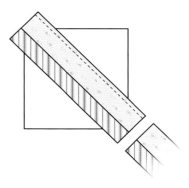

3. Sew the strips together using a ¼"-wide seam allowance. Fold the second strip open onto the stabilizer, and using a silk setting on the iron, press the strip.

4. Continue randomly adding strips in this manner until the stabilizer square is covered. After all the strips have been sewn, gently remove the stabilizer.

5. To square up the blocks, place them one at a time on your cutting mat, right side up. Using a rotary cutter and a 6½" square ruler with a 45° line, center the ruler in the middle of the block with the 45° line parallel to the closest diagonal seam. The fabric should extend beyond the ruler on all sides as shown. Trim all four sides to make a 6½" square. Make a total of 30 blocks.

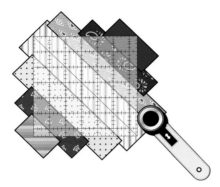

A Word about Stabilizers

If you're going to make a quilt top that will be handled, such as a table runner or a larger quilt, you'll want to remove the stabilizer from the blocks. The quilt shown was intended to be a wall hanging, so I left the stabilizer on the back of the blocks for a flatter, crisper surface. You can achieve this look with a little less stiffness by using an iron-on interfacing. Press the interfacing on the wrong side of each tie strip before sewing it to the stabilizer square. Then remove the stabilizer square once the block is completed.

EMBELLISHING

1. Arrange the blocks in six rows of five blocks each on a design wall or other large surface. Rotate every other block 90° so that the strips form diagonal lines across the quilt as shown in the photo on page 77 and the assembly diagram on page 81.

Photo Finish

Once I've laid out the blocks and I'm pleased with the placement, I take a digital photo of the layout. When I pick the blocks up to sew on the bias strips, I can refer to the photo to find where the block belongs in the layout. This works through all the finishing stages, from sewing on the bias strips to sewing the blocks into rows and completing the quilt top.

2. Place a bias strip across the opposite diagonal of a block. Pin in place and trim the strip even with the edge of the block. Repeat with a second color bias strip as shown.

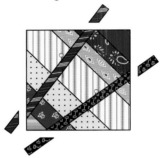

3. Repeat with the remaining blocks to pin and trim two bias strips to each block.

4. Sew the bias strips onto each block using an invisible stitch. To make an invisible stitch, bring the needle up underneath the bias strip along the folded edge and through the bottom layer *only*. Slide the needle between the layers of the strip for about ½"; then bring it back down through the strip and the block. Repeat the stitch along both sides of the bias strip.

Assembling the Quilt Top

1. Referring to your photo, return the completed blocks to your design wall and carefully examine the layout to make sure that each block is placed correctly.

2. Sew the blocks together into rows. Press the seam allowances in opposite directions from row to row. Sew the rows together and press the seam allowances in one direction.

Finishing

Refer to the finishing techniques on pages 23–25 for detailed instructions if needed.

1. Layer the quilt top, backing, and batting and baste the layers together.

2. Hand or machine quilt as desired.

3. Using the gray and navy 2¼"-wide binding strips, prepare the binding and sew it to your quilt.

Quilt assembly

Fresh Breeze

Pieced and machine quilted by Leah Fehr

Finished quilt: 16½" x 40½"

Finished small block: 4" x 4"

Finished large block: 12" x 12"

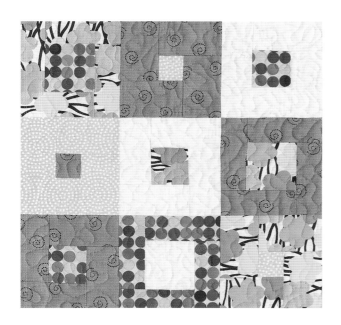

MATERIALS

Yardage is based on 42"-wide fabric. Fat quarters measure 18" x 21".

½ yard of yellow print for blocks and border
⅜ yard of blue floral for blocks and binding
1 fat quarter of cream print for blocks
1 fat quarter of blue swirl print for blocks
1 fat quarter of blue dotted fabric for blocks
1⅜ yard of fabric for backing
23" x 47" piece of batting
Pencil or chalk marker

CUTTING

From the yellow print, cut:
2 strips, 2½" x 40½"
2 strips, 2½" x 16½"
1 square, 6½" x 6½"
4 rectangles, 2" x 3"
2 squares, 1½" x 1½"

From the blue dotted fabric, cut:
4 rectangles, 3½" x 9½"
4 rectangles, 1½" x 3½"
1 square, 2½" x 2½"
2 squares, 2" x 2"

From the cream print, cut:
4 rectangles, 3½" x 9½"
1 square, 2½" x 2½"
8 rectangles, 1¾" x 3¼"

From the blue swirl print, cut:
1 square, 6½" x 6½"
4 rectangles, 2" x 3"
4 rectangles, 1¾" x 3¼"
4 rectangles, 1½" x 3½"
1 square, 1½" x 1½"

From the blue floral, cut:
4 binding strips, 2¼" x 42"
1 square, 2½" x 2½"
4 rectangles, 2" x 3"
1 square, 2" x 2"
4 rectangles, 1½" x 3½"

MAKING THE BLOCKS

1. With right sides together, align one edge of a blue dotted 3½" x 9½" rectangle with the yellow 6½" square as shown. Beginning at the aligned edge, sew the rectangle to the square with a partial seam, stopping about 1" from the square's edge. Press the seam allowances toward the yellow square.

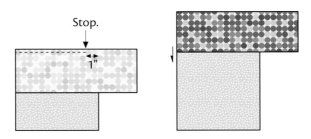

2. Sew a blue dotted 3½" x 9½" rectangle to the left side of the square as shown. Press the seam allowances toward the yellow square. Continue sewing blue dotted rectangles around the square in the same manner. Complete the partial seam stitched in step 1 to complete a large block. Press the seam allowances toward the yellow square.

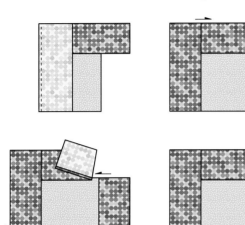

3. In the same manner, sew together the cream 3½" x 9½" rectangles and the blue swirl 6½" square to make a second large block.

4. Repeat steps 1 and 2, sewing the squares and rectangles together in the combinations listed below to make a total of nine small blocks:
- one yellow 1½" square and four blue floral 2" x 3" rectangles
- one yellow 1½" square and four blue swirl 2" x 3" rectangles
- one blue swirl 1½" square and four yellow 2" x 3" rectangles
- one blue dotted 2" square and four cream 1¾" x 3¼" rectangles
- one blue floral 2" square and four cream 1¾" x 3¼" rectangles
- one blue dotted 2" square and four blue swirl 1¾" x 3¼" rectangles
- one blue floral 2½" square and four blue swirl 1½" x 3½" rectangles

- one cream 2½" square and four blue dotted 1½" x 3½" rectangles
- one blue dotted 2½" square and four blue floral 1½" x 3½" rectangles

Assembling the Quilt Top

1. Arrange the nine small blocks in three rows of three blocks each.

2. Sew the blocks together into rows. Press the seam allowances in opposite directions from row to row. Sew the rows together to make a large block. Press the seam allowances in one direction. The large block should measure 12½" square.

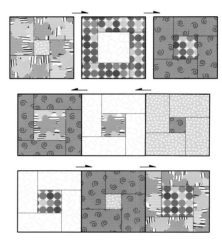

3. Arrange the blocks as shown in the quilt assembly diagram on page 85 with the block from step 2 in the middle. Sew the blocks together. Press the seam allowances in one direction.

Adding the Border

1. On the wrong side of quilt center, and using a pencil or chalk marker, mark each corner ¼" from the raw edge as shown in preparation for making mitered corners.

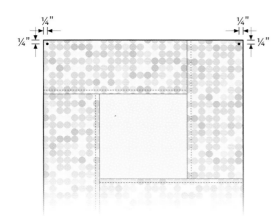

2. Fold the quilt center in half, right sides together, vertically and horizontally. Finger-press to mark the center of each side of the quilt center. Fold the yellow 2½"-wide strips in half, wrong sides together. Finger-press one side to mark the center of the strip.

3. With right sides together, place a creased 40½"-long strip on one long side of the quilt center, matching the center creases as shown; pin in place. Pin a strip on the opposite side of the quilt in the same manner.

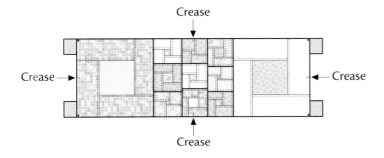

Crease
Crease → ← Crease
Crease

4. With the quilt center on top, sew the strips to the quilt, starting and stopping at the ¼" marks with a small backstitch. Press the seam allowances toward the quilt center.

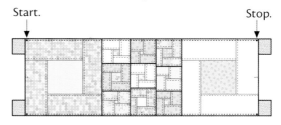

Start.　　　Stop.

5. Repeat steps 3 and 4 to sew the 16½"-long strips to the quilt center. The unstitched ends of the strips will extend beyond the quilt.

6. Fold one end of the quilt diagonally, right sides together and align the edges of the strips. Draw a diagonal line from the corner of the strip to the seam line. Stitch exactly on the marked line, sewing from the inner corner to the outer edge to make a mitered corner. Trim the seam allowance to ¼" and press to one side. Miter the remaining corners in the same manner. Refer to "Mitered Square Block," step 8, on page 33 as needed for further guidance.

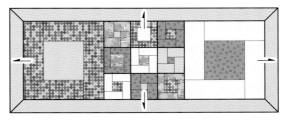

Quilt assembly

Finishing

Refer to the finishing techniques on pages 23–25 for detailed instructions if needed.

1. Layer the quilt top, backing, and batting and baste the layers together.

2. Hand or machine quilt as desired.

3. Using the blue floral 2¼"-wide binding strips, prepare the binding and sew it to your quilt.

Get carried away by the current with this fluid, contemporary bed quilt.

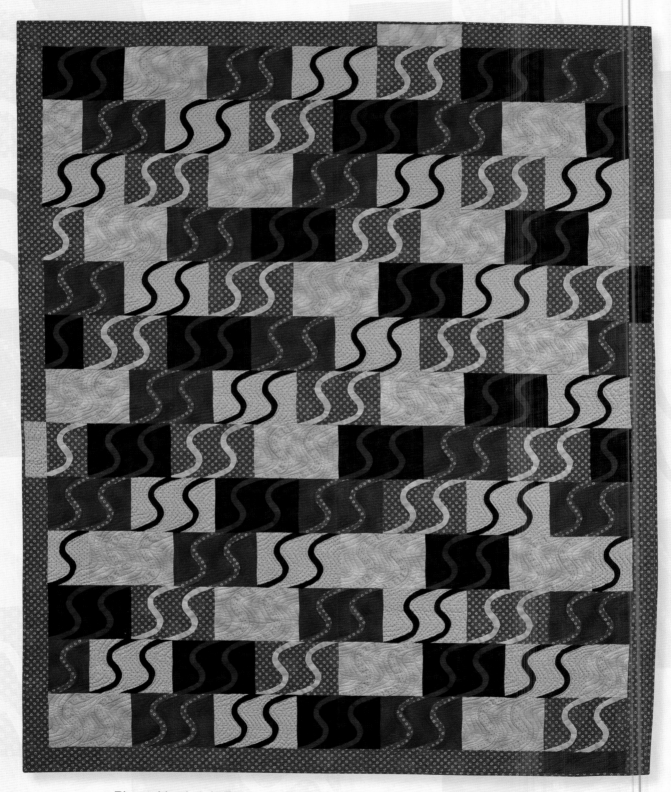

Pieced by Leah Fehr and machine quilted by Rosalie Davenport

Finished quilt: 68½" x 83½" • Finished large block: 9" x 6" • Finished small block: 4½" x 6"

Pacific Waves

MATERIALS

Yardage is based on 42"-wide fabric.

3 yards of red dotted fabric for blocks, appliqués, border, and binding

1¾ yards of mottled red fabric for blocks and appliqués

1¾ yards of mottled navy fabric for blocks and appliqués

1¾ yards of light blue print for blocks and appliqués

1¾ yards of khaki print for blocks and appliqués

5½ yards of fabric for backing

75" x 90" piece of batting

6 yards of 16"-wide fusible web

Red, navy blue, light blue, and khaki thread

Pencil or chalk marker

⅛" wooden dowel

PREPARING FUSIBLE APPLIQUÉS

Referring to "Fusible Appliqué" on page 18 and using the pattern on page 91, trace 182 swirls onto the paper side of fusible web. Nestle the swirls together on the fusible web so you can fuse them as a single unit to the wrong side of the fabrics. Fuse 38 swirls onto the red dotted fabric, 35 swirls onto the mottled red fabric, 36 swirls onto the mottled navy fabric, 36 swirls onto the light blue print, and 37 swirls onto the khaki print.

CUTTING

From the red dotted fabric, cut:

7 border strips, 3" x 42"

8 binding strips, 2¼" x 42"

17 rectangles, 6½" x 9½"

2 rectangles, 5" x 6½"

38 swirls, prepared with fusible web

From the mottled red fabric, cut:

18 rectangles, 6½" x 9½"

2 rectangles, 5" x 6½"

1 rectangle, 3" x 12"

35 swirls, prepared with fusible web

From the mottled navy fabric, cut:

16 rectangles, 6½" x 9½"

3 rectangles, 5" x 6½"

1 rectangle, 3" x 9"

36 swirls, prepared with fusible web

From the light blue print, cut:

17 rectangles, 6½" x 9½"

3 rectangles, 5" x 6½"

1 rectangle, 3" x 11½"

36 swirls, prepared with fusible web

From the khaki print, cut:
17 rectangles, 6½" x 9½"
2 rectangles, 5" x 6½"
1 rectangle, 3" x 7½"
37 swirls, prepared with fusible web

Appliquéing the Blocks

1. Fold each red dotted 6½" x 9½" rectangle in half and lightly crease to mark the center of each long side. Remove the paper backing from two light blue swirls. Place the swirls on the red dotted rectangle, taking care to position the pieces using the center marks as shown. When satisfied with the placement, fuse the swirls in place. Machine stitch a narrow zigzag or blanket stitch along both sides of each swirl with matching thread. Repeat to make a total of 17 red dotted large swirl blocks.

Crease

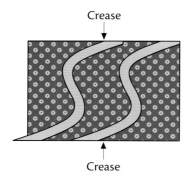

Crease

2. Remove the paper backing from one light blue swirl. Place the swirl on a red dotted 5" x 6½" rectangle, so that the swirl's top edge hangs over the top right side of the rectangle ⅛" as shown. When satisfied with the placement, fuse the swirl in place. Machine stitch a narrow zigzag or blanket stitch along both sides of the swirl with matching thread. Repeat to make a total of two red dotted small swirl blocks.

⅛"

3. In the same manner as steps 1 and 2, appliqué the red dotted swirls to the mottled red rectangles to make 18 large swirl blocks and 2 small swirl blocks. Appliqué the mottled red swirls to the mottled navy rectangles to make 16 large swirl blocks and 3 small swirl blocks. Appliqué the khaki swirls to the light blue rectangles to make 17 large swirl blocks and 3 small swirl blocks. Then appliqué the mottled navy swirls to the khaki rectangles to make 17 large swirl blocks and 2 small swirl blocks.

Exact Fit

Positioning the swirl appliqués goes faster if you don't have to mark the centerline on each rectangle. Mark the rectangle's centerline on a 12" square ruler by placing a 7½"-long piece of masking tape vertically along the 4¾" mark, as shown. Lay one large rectangle on top of the square ruler, aligning one short side with the right edge of the ruler. You should be able to see the tape along the top and bottom edges of the rectangle. If not, adjust the tape or the rectangle until you do. Now when you align each rectangle with the ruler's right edge, the center of the rectangle is already marked and you're able to lay the two swirls in place quickly and easily.

4¾"

7½"

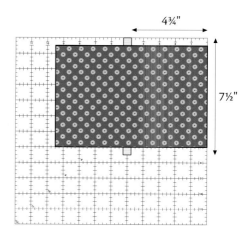

Assembling the Quilt top

1. Arrange the large and small swirl blocks in thirteen rows as shown in the quilt assembly diagram.

2. Sew the blocks together into rows. Press the seam allowances in opposite directions from row to row. Sew the rows together and press the seam allowances in one direction. The quilt top should measure 63½" x 78½", including seam allowances.

Quilt assembly

Adding the Border

1. Refer to "Folded Seams" on page 19 for detailed instructions. On the right side of the khaki 3" x 7½" rectangle, place marks on each long side at the 2" and 5" points. Mark the light blue 3" x 11½" rectangle at the 1½", 3", 6½", and 8" points. Mark the mottled red 3" x 12" rectangle at the 2", 3½", 5", 8", and 9½" points, and then mark the mottled navy 3" x 9" rectangle at the 1½", 3", 4½", 6", and 7½" points.

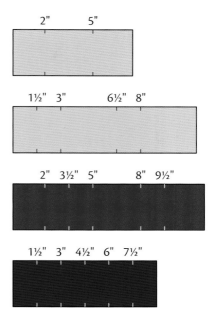

2. Using the wooden dowel, fold and pin each rectangle around the dowel so that the first pair of marks is aligned on the back of the dowel. Sew ⅛" from the edge of the dowel using its straight edge as a guideline as shown. Remove the dowel and press the fold to one side.

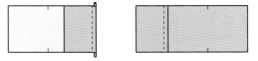

3. Repeat step 2 to sew the remaining folds on each marked rectangle. Press the folds in the same direction after sewing each fold. The khaki and mottled navy rectangles should each measure 3" x 6½", including the seam allowances. The light blue and mottled red rectangles should each measure 3" x 9½", including seam allowances.

4. Referring to "Borders" on page 22, sew the red dotted 3"-wide border strips together end to end. From the long strip, cut the following lengths:

- one strip, 57" long
- one strip, 48½" long
- one strip, 42½" long
- one strip, 39" long
- one strip, 30½" long
- one strip, 24½" long
- one strip, 21" long
- one square, 3" x 3"

5. Assemble the four border strips using the red dotted 3"-wide strips and square and the khaki, mottled navy, light blue, and mottled red folded-seam rectangles as follows. Press the seam allowances in one direction.

Top border: 39"-long red dotted strip, light blue rectangle, 21"-long red dotted strip.

Bottom border: 57"-long red dotted strip, mottled red rectangle, 3" red dotted square.

Right border: 48½"-long red dotted strip, mottled navy rectangle, 24½"-long red dotted strip.

Left border: 42½"-long red dotted strip, khaki rectangle, 30½"-long red dotted strip.

6. Measure the left and right pieced borders. If necessary, trim them to fit the length of the quilt, which should be 78½". Sew the borders to the sides of the quilt. Press the seam allowances toward the border.

7. Measure the top and bottom pieced borders. They should measure 68½". Sew the borders to the quilt. Press the seam allowances toward the border.

FINISHING

Refer to the finishing techniques on pages 23–25 for detailed instructions if needed.

1. Layer the quilt top, backing, and batting and baste the layers together.

2. Hand or machine quilt as desired.

3. Using the red dotted 2¼"-wide binding strips, prepare the binding and sew it to your quilt.

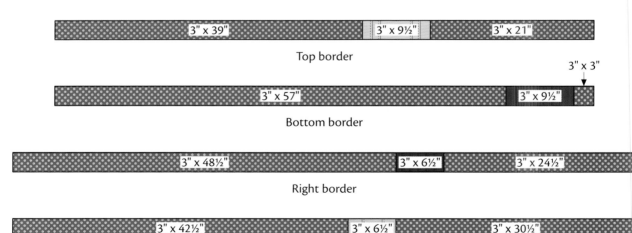

3" x 39" 3" x 9½" 3" x 21"

Top border

3" x 3"

3" x 57" 3" x 9½"

Bottom border

3" x 48½" 3" x 6½" 3" x 24½"

Right border

3" x 42½" 3" x 6½" 3" x 30½"

Left border

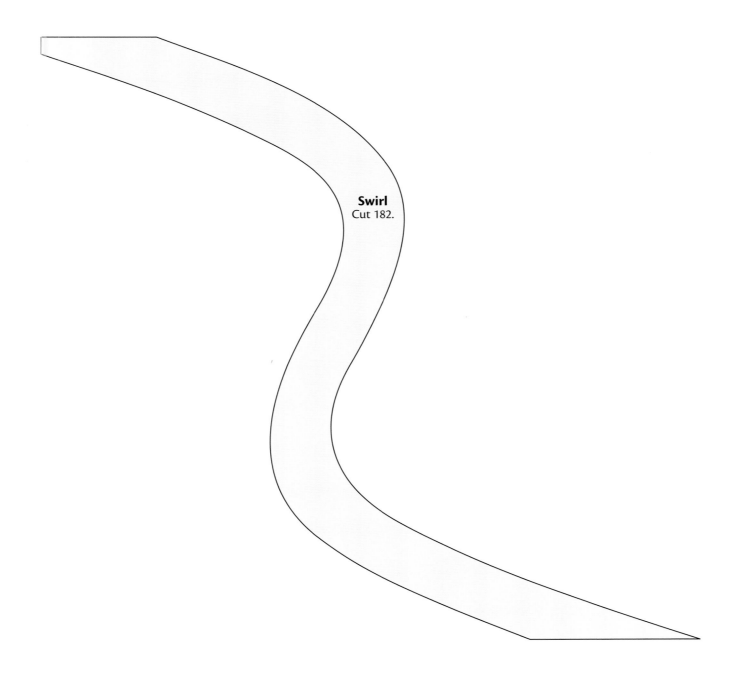

Swirl
Cut 182.

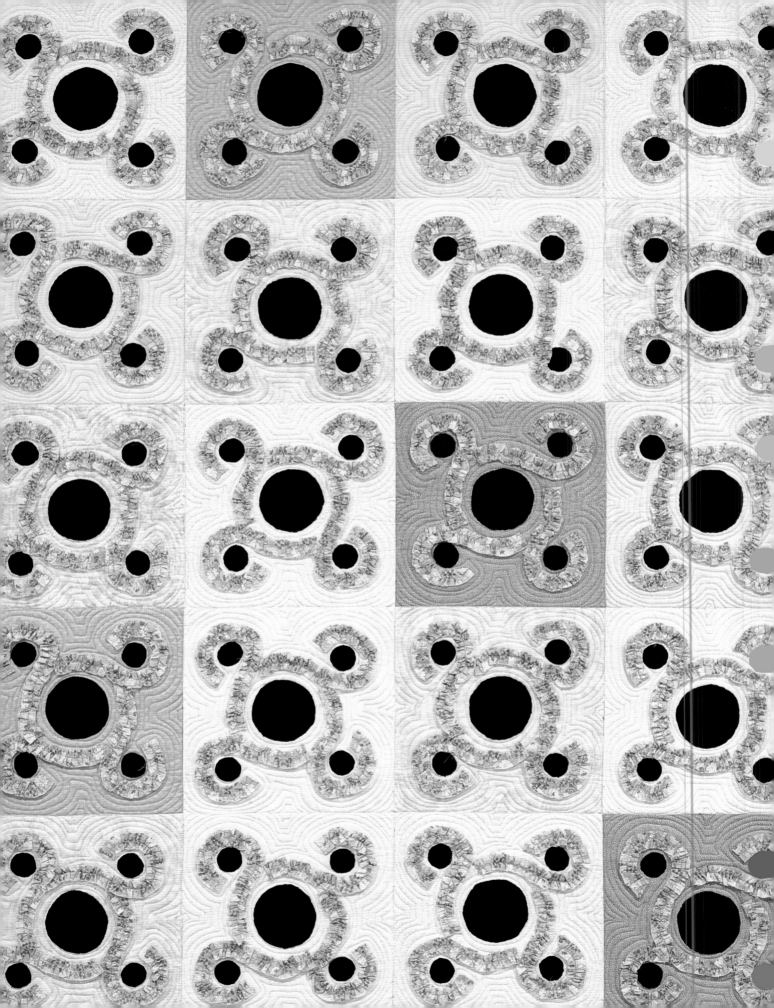

About the Author

LEAH FEHR and her grandmother collaborated on her first quilt when she was 12 years old. With the aid of a new sewing machine given to her as a college graduation gift from her parents, she has finished many more quilts since. Leah worked as an instruction writer for the *Better Homes and Gardens* Quilt Group in Des Moines, Iowa, for two years before she left for another collaboration—marriage. She and her husband, a chief officer on a cruise line, divide their time between the ship and their home in Switzerland. This is her first book.

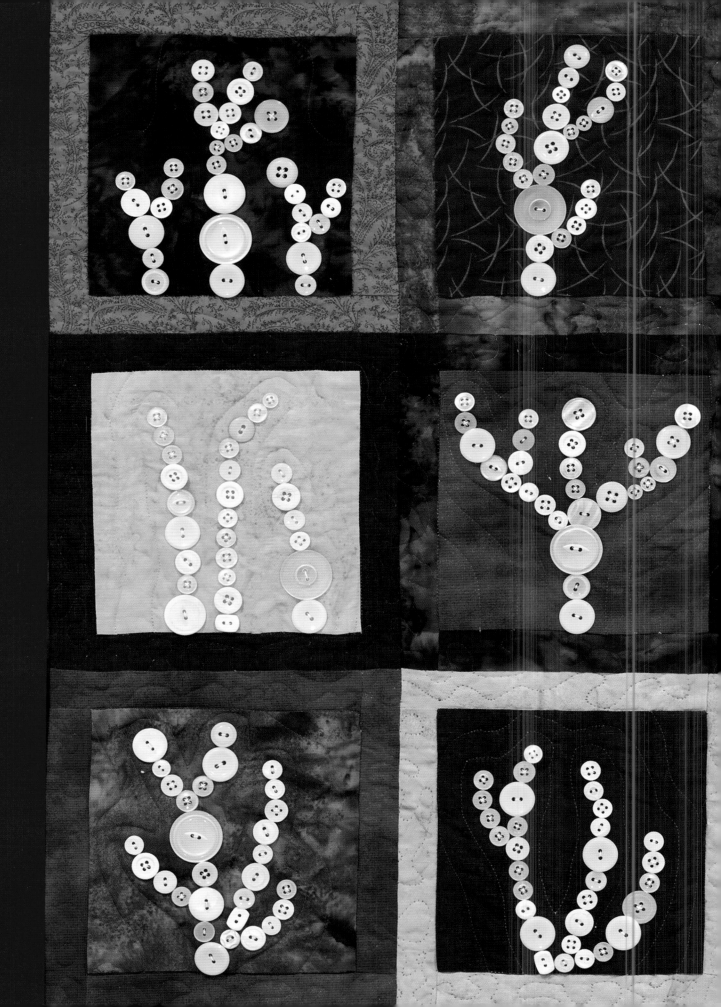